D0095774

How To

~~Survive~~

Win

The

Immigration

Debate

How to ~~Survive~~ *Win* The Immigration Debate

How to ~~Survive~~ Win The Immigration Debate

The Federation for American Immigration Reform
Washington, D.C.

The Federation for American Immigration Reform
1666 Connecticut Avenue NW #400
Washington DC 20009

ISBN 0-935776-24-9

Contents

How to ~~Survive~~ *Win* the
Immigration Debate

How to S̶u̶r̶v̶i̶v̶e̶ Win the Immigration Debate

About the Publisher

The Federation for American Immigration Reform (FAIR) is a national, non-profit, public interest organization of concerned citizens working to reform our nation's immigration policy. FAIR seeks to improve border security, to stop illegal immigration, and to promote an immigration "time out" or pause to reduce levels as far as practicable. FAIR is the largest and most effective organization in the United States dedicated exclusively to immigration issues. It is financially supported by some 70,000 members and 40 foundations nationwide. FAIR is a tax-exempt organization (and not a private foundation) under section 501(c)(3) of the Internal Revenue Code.

Federation for American Immigration Reform
1666 Connecticut Avenue NW #400
Washington DC 20009

Authored by Scipio Garling.

How to ~~Survive~~ *Win* the Immigration Debate

What is this Manual for?

This manual is geared toward helping you, who already understand the need for immigration reform, make the case to others, who may not yet understand.

It should also help you argue the matter against those who are opposed to immigration reform.

It presumes some familiarity with immigration terms and the immigration system. If it refers to parts of the immigration system that are not familiar to you, consider reading the Appendix, *Understanding the Immigration System*.

If you are not yet convinced of the need for immigration reform, beware; you just may change your mind by the time you are done reading.

HOW TO MAKE
YOUR OWN
IMMIGRATION
ARGUMENTS

How to Make Your Own Immigration Arguments

We have all been in debates where we knew we were right—we knew what the facts were and the facts were on our side—yet we still seemed to be losing the debate.

That is because mere facts are not enough. *Facts* need the larger context of an overall *argument*. Facts without arguments are like words without sentences; they signify something, but it's hard to tell what without structure or context.

As an immigration reformer, you probably get facts about immigration every month; from FAIR's newsletter or website (http://www.fairus.org), from your local reform group newsletter, even from your hometown newspaper. The focus of this book to help you get a handle on the arguments you need to use more persuasively whatever facts come your way.

The Overall Argument for Immigration Reform

There are as many ways to structure the argument for immigration reform as there are immigration reformers. Every way has its pros and its cons. What we have tried to do is synthesize years of experience of immigration reformers in debating the issue into an overall argument that should work anytime you find yourself discussing the issue. While some unique circumstances may require a different approach, we think this one, by and large, is your best bet.

So as not to bewilder your audience with the myriad of points in favor of immigration reform, it helps to groups those points into broad categories, or arguments. The arguments for immigration reform (or against the present immigration policy, if you prefer to look at it that way) come in four flavors:

> **Traditional.** Our present immigration policy is not consistent with our immigration tradition.
> **Economic.** Immigration is not good for the economy.
> **Social.** Too much immigration causes unhealthy social strain.
> **Population/Environmental.** Immigration is an environmental/population problem.

Ideally, whenever you present the case for immigration reform, you should touch on all these areas. Individually, they leave holes for opponents (or simply the skeptical) to dodge through. But, as a team, these four points make a nearly unshakable case for immigration reform.

Naturally, some points will resonate stronger with particular audiences. A Sierra Club member, for example, is more likely to be receptive to your environmental concerns than a real estate developer. When you find yourself discussing the issue, you may want to lean toward the arguments most likely to appeal to the interests of your audience.

While it is not absolutely necessary, it is helpful to make the arguments in the above sequence. Your argument would go roughly as follows:

- present immigration policy violates our immigration tradition;
- even if it didn't, it is damaging to the economy;
- even if it weren't, it causes social strain;
- and even if you disregard that, immigration drives population growth and environmental degradation.

For example, if you were, say, arguing the issue at the bus stop and had limited time to get your points across, you might make the case the following way.

Traditional. Our present immigration policy is not consistent with our immigration tradition. We are taking over 900,000 legal immigrants each year (and about 300,000 illegal), which is many times more than we received historically. Besides, our tradition is about taking in immigrants when we needed them for our economy, which we certainly don't now.

Economic. Immigration is not good for the economy. How can importing almost one million mostly poor, low-skilled people into the country every year be good for the economy?

Social. Too much immigration is unhealthy for society. We are bringing people in faster than they assimilate. Thus, the size of the unassimilated population grows. The larger the unassimilated population, the greater the chance for friction and conflict.

Population/Environmental. Immigration is an environmental/population problem. Immigration is responsible for half of population growth in the U.S. Without immigration, the U.S. population will stabilize. Under our present immigration policy, the U.S. population will grow unceasingly. As the number of people goes up, the amount of environmental degradation they cause goes up, too.

Some audiences will respond better to some points than others; this is something you should keep in mind when deciding how to present the case for immigration reform. But the best argument you can make will touch on all these points.

Often when you are arguing the issue, you will barely have enough time to make the four points as briefly as above. Other times, however, you may have the opportunity to make a more detailed case.

Examples of more detailed arguments follow. There are three arguments for each of the four "flavors" above. After each set of arguments, we have included a selection of quotes that you might use in writing arguments of your own.

In the following selections, you will probably notice facts, figures, and points that appear more than once. This is intentional; it demonstrates how information can be used in more than one argument. In fact, having a reasonable amount of overlap between some of your arguments helps give them the feeling of being interlocked and cohesive.

You may also notice that there are different types of evidence used to support the arguments:

- Dense **statistical evidence** and similar facts and figures serve, as it were, as the heavy artillery of argument; they take some time to set up and get across, but have quite an impact when they hit the target.

- **Anecdotal evidence**, that is, stories of local impacts, incidents, and quotes are the infantry, making your case one-by-one, painstakingly but effectively.

- Broad **commonsense assertions** can be thought of as the cavalry, swiftly striking at the heart of the issue, and often saving the day.

No one kind of evidence will make your case as strong as you want it; usually, a combination works best. So, in ideal circumstances, you will be able to use all three types of evidence when making your own arguments for immigration reform.

The Tradition Argument

Tradition arguments address one of the basic myths about immigration in America: that to reduce immigration violates our country's "tradition of immigration." This objection is one of the first that crops up in the debate on immigration reform, and it is not confined to hard-core opponents. Many well-meaning people hold this view.

But you have an advantage: You know more. They probably haven't thought about how much greater is the amount of immigration we are receiving now, and how different the country is now from 200 or even 100 years ago. For that reason, their view is a gut reaction, not a well informed opinion.

How do you deal with such people? Give them the history; give them the truth. Comparing what went before to what is happening now is often very effective at answering their objections.

What follows are three ways to make a tradition argument in favor of immigration reform. While you will seldom have the opportunity to go into the detail you will find here, you definitely want to confront the tradition objections head-on every time you discuss the issue. You may want to tackle them first thing, too. For many people, if you can't shake their hold on those objections, you will be unable to get any further in explaining the need for immigration reform to them.

Tradition Argument No. 1:
The Not-So-Great Wave
or
Why Turn-of-the-Century Immigration is No Model for Immigration Today

Supporters of today's hyper-immigration like to claim that we should not be concerned about it, because it is no worse than the Great Wave, which (we are repeatedly told) was good for America.

But the Great Wave of immigration at the turn of the century was a great burden on society. Immigration caused explosive population growth in the inner city.[1] A congressional study found that new arrivals were three times more likely than natives to be on welfare in 1909, comprised more than half the people on welfare, constituted one third of the patients in public hospitals, and that thirty-three percent of them were illiterate. A national commission studied the impact of immigration for five years and concluded in 1911 that it was contributing to low wages and poor working conditions.[2] In the words of contemporary historian and scholar, Frederick Jackson Turner:

> The immigrant of the preceding period was
> assimilated with comparative ease...but the
> free lands that made the process of absorption

---

[1] By 1920, new immigrants comprised 44 percent of New York's population, 41 percent of Cleveland's, 39 percent of Newark's, and 24 percent of the populations in Boston, Buffalo, Detroit, Philadelphia, and Pittsburgh, and had created the most densely populated slums in the world. *From Open Door to Dutch Door*, Michael LeMay, 1987.

[2] *The Case Against Immigration*, Roy Beck, 1996.

easy have gone. The immigration is becoming increasingly more difficult of assimilation. Its competition with American labor under existing conditions may give increased power to the producer, but the effects upon American well-being are dangerous in the extreme. [3]

Many immigration supporters would have you believe that the reason that the Great Wave of immigration was ended was prejudice and racism. But, in fact:

> The real objection has nothing to do with the composition of our immigration stream, nor with the characteristics of the individuals or races composing it. ... The real objection to immigration lies in the changed conditions that have come about in the United States themselves. These conditions now dominate and control the tendencies that immigration manifests. At the present time, they are giving the country a surplus of cheap labour—a greater supply than our industries and manufacturing enterprises need. In consequence, this over-supply has brought into play among our industrial toilers the great law of competition. This economic law is controlled by the more recent immigrant because of his immediate necessity to secure employment and his ability to sell his labour at a low price—to work for a low wage. Against the

---

[3] *Chicago Record-Herald*, September 25, 1901.

operation of this law the native worker and the
earlier immigrant are unable to defend
themselves. It is affecting detrimentally the
standard of living of hundreds of thousands of
workers — workers, too, who are also
citizens, fathers, husbands.[4]

It was the effect of immigration on wages and working
conditions that finally rallied the labor unions to back
numerical restrictions in the early 20th century. The effect
was so clearly negative that even the cities whose voters were
more and more likely to be immigrants realized the need to
cut immigration:

Urban America moved strongly into the pro-
immigration camp as its ever-increasing
foreign-born constituency gained the vote.
But even in the nation's largest cities, the
economic impact of immigrants on the
economic status of native-born workers
heavily impacted pro-immigration sentiment.
And it was the withering away of the urban
pro-immigration vote that ultimately closed
the door.[5]

The problems of high immigration today cannot be
dismissed because we survived the Great Wave. That ignores
not only the problems at the turn of century but also the fact

---

[4] *The Immigrant Invasion*, Frank Julian Warne, 1913.

[5] *The Political Economy of Immigration Restriction in the United States,
1890–1921*, Claudia Goldin, National Bureau of Economic Research,
1993.

it was immigration restrictions that saved the day. Just as the solution to problems of the Great Wave was a reduction of immigration to normal, manageable levels, so too the answer to today's "new wave" is immigration reform. The lesson that we should learn from our history is that, rather than emulating the excesses of the Great Wave, we should be emulating the wisdom of those who ended it before it swamped the country.

Tradition Argument No. 2:
Immigration, Now and Then
or
Why Today's Immigration is a
Worse Problem Than
the Great Wave

Supporters of today's hyper-immigration like to claim that we should not be concerned about it, because it is no worse than the Great Wave of immigration at the turn of the last century. But in fact, because times have changed greatly in the last one hundred years, immigration now is much more out-of-sync with our country's needs than it was at the turn of the last century.

In the economy of the late 1800s, low-skilled workers were employable. New mechanical devices and processes were being introduced that did away with the need for workers with special industrial skills and know-how. As the U.S. Industrial Commission pointed out: "The fact that machinery and the division of labor opens a place for the unskilled immigrants makes it possible not only to get the advantages of machinery, but also to get the advantages of cheap labor."[6] Turn-of-the-century technology created the need for unskilled workers; but modern technology requires skilled workers, not unskilled ones. Yet, in 1995, only 5 percent of legal immigrants were admitted as skilled workers.[7]

Before 1900, there may have been some marginal

---

[6]U.S. Congress, House Industrial Commission, 1901, Vol. 14, pp. 313-314.

[7]The share of skilled workers was greater than that even a hundred years ago, at around 13 percent (*The Dilemma of American Immigration: Beyond the Golden Door*, Barry Chiswick, 1983.)

fiscal gain from immigrants. The U.S. Treasury Department calculated in the late 1800s that each immigrant was worth, on average, $800 (in 1870s dollars) to the economy. Today, the estimated annual net *cost* of each immigrant, on average, is $2700 (in 1990s dollars).

At the turn of **last** century, having relatives in the United States made it logistically easier to immigrate here; it did not, however, guarantee that you would be admitted. At the turn of **this** century, having relatives in the United States makes you legally eligible to immigrate, and guarantees you eventual admission.[8] In 1995, 82 percent of legal immigrants were admitted simply because they had a relative here. Due to the eligibility of the foreign relatives of immigrants, there is a line of three and a half million aliens waiting and eligible for admission as immigrants to the United States.

Then, immigrants' stay in the U.S. was often temporary; today's immigrants are here to stay:

> "the majority of immigrants to the United States at the turn of the century intended their stay to be only temporary until, after a few years of work, they could save enough money to return home to an improved position for themselves and their families. ... Although the majority of new immigrants permanently settled in America, a significant number left (with a departure rate of 35 percent for Croatians, Poles, Serbs, and Slovenes; 40 percent for Greeks; and more than 50 percent for Hungarians, Slovaks, and Italians; the rate

---

[8]The process is called "chain migration".

among Asian immigrants was much higher—more than two thirds)."[9]

The Immigration and Naturalization Service estimates that the rate of return from 1900 to 1904 was over 37 percent[10]; in the 1990s, the rate of return of the immigrant flow is a much lower 15 percent.[11]

Ethnic ghettoization and its retardation of assimilation is more serious now than a hundred years ago. At that time, "Only rarely did a single ethnic group dominate an area of several city blocks, and even then many immigrants moved out of such areas." Now, ethnic enclaves are huge and growing; in the city of Miami, for example, fifty percent of the population speaks English poorly or not at all, and seventy-three percent speak a language other than English at home.[12]

During those frontier days, we had a vast empty country and states starved for people:

> "After the Civil War, practically all the states and territories west of the Mississippi River encouraged immigration. They set up immigration bureaus and put advertisements in western European newspapers telling the advantages of settling in their areas. Men

---

[9] *The Tyranny of Change: America in the Progressive Era, 1890–1920*, John Whiteclay Chambers, 1992.

[10] "The Elusive Exodus: Emigration from the United States," *Population Trends and Public Policy*, No. 8, March 1985, by Robert Warren of INS Statistics.

[11] Center for Immigration Studies, January, 1997.

[12] 1990 Census.

were hired as immigration agents by the states and territories and were sent to Europe to direct the immigrants to Missouri, Minnesota, or Iowa, as the case might be. The railroads, too, spent large sums of money in efforts to attract immigrants to their lands ."[13]

Now, our country is increasingly congested and communities pass ordinances to limit ·the growth of their populations. In 1900, the number of people per square mile in the United States was 25.6; in 1997 it was 76 people per square mile—three times greater population density.[14]

U.S. Population Density
1790 to present

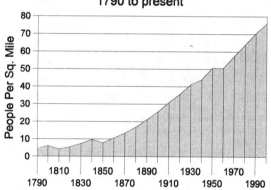

---

[13]*American Immigration*, Edward Hartmann, 1979.

[14]Even at the turn of last century, it was known that era of needed expansion in the U.S. was at an end. At the 1893 meeting of the American Historical Society, Frederick Jackson Turner began his paper on "The Significance of the Frontier in American History" by noting that the Bureau of the Census had just announced that there was no longer a continuous line of free unsettled land visible on the U.S. map. The American "frontier" had closed. [*Alien Nation*, Peter Brimelow, 1995.]

15

TRADITION ARGUMENT NO. 3:
IMMIGRATION LEVELS IN PERSPECTIVE
OR
THE TRUTH IS IN THE NUMBERS

Some people support present immigration policy naively, thinking that the level of immigration we are receiving now is what the United States has always had. But the present level of immigration is far above historical levels and is **not** consistent with our immigration tradition. A few comparisons help to put the present level of legal immigration into perspective.[15]

- During the first fifty years after Independence, the United States received about 710,000 immigrants— in 1996 alone the United States admitted 912,000.
- During the first century or so of our country (1776 to 1884), we received about two immigrants a day; in the 1990s, we are admitting two immigrants **a minute.**
- In the last fifteen years, the United States has admitted more immigrants than it did in the previous **fifty** years.
- The level of legal immigration has **doubled** in the last twenty years.
- In the 1990s, we have admitted enough new immigrants to make two new cities the size of Washington, D.C., **every year**.
- The 1990 Immigration Act increased legal immigration by **forty percent.**

---

[15] All statistics from the INS Statistics Division and the U.S. Census Bureau.

- There are **twenty-five million** immigrants already living in the United States; this is a larger population than 49 of the 50 states.

Average Annual Immigration Levels in American History:

1776–1884	14,200
1845–1900	322,000
1901–1914	923,000
1915–1965	220,000
1966–1988	482,000
1989–present	1,122,000

Half of all immigrants come from **just ten** countries:

Mexico
China
The Philippines
The Dominican Republic
Vietnam
India
Poland
The Ukraine
El Salvador
Ireland

Other Quotes About Tradition

"The 1965 Immigration Act, the great reform bill, was passed amidst an almost unbelievable amount of ignorance about what its own impact would be. You can read the thousands of pages of testimony over the 1965 Act and not find very many pages discussing, for example, immigration from the western hemisphere, which was considered to be a non-issue. No numerical limitations were placed in that 1965 Act on immigration from the western hemisphere because it was not a problem. It was not even a potential problem to those who wrote the Act."
Elliott Abrams, Assistant Secretary of State for Latin American Affairs under President Reagan.

"In 1893 Frederick Jackson Turner announced that the American frontier was closed. 'Closing the frontier', said Turner, was 'the first period of American history.' A century later, it may be time to close the second period of American history with the announcement that the U.S. is no longer an 'immigration country.'"
Peter Brimelow, "Time to Rethink Immigration?", *National Review*, June 22, 1992.

"Critics of current U.S. immigration policy worry about what to call themselves. They think their inability to get a public hearing is partly because they don't, quite literally, have a good name. ...I suggest that the critics of immigration adopt a name that has a long and honorable role in American history. They should call themselves 'Patriots'."
Peter Brimelow, *Alien Nation*, p. 254 (1995).

"There was not thought of any great wave of immigration 30 years ago. The immigration bill (in 1965) was sold as not bringing in any more numbers, but it did. And the composition of the numbers changed dramatically. Suddenly, 75 percent of new immigrants were racial and ethnic minorities. When affirmative action was begun, these persons were rolled into that program. And that's because affirmative action was set up to be triggered by ethnicity and race, not nationality or citizenship."
James Robb, senior researcher at The Social Contract, *BorderLine*, February 20, 1996.

"It is a commonplace of American life that immigrants have made our country great and continue to make a very important contribution to the fabric of American life. But... under the pressure we face today, we can't afford to lose control of our borders, or to take on new financial burdens, at a time when we are not adequately providing for the jobs, the health care, and the education of our own people. Therefore, immigration must be a priority for this administration."
President Bill Clinton, *Christian Science Monitor*, June 21, 1993.

"The time has come to risk being politically incorrect, to take off the blindfolds, to think the unthinkable and speak the unspeakable: There are too many people coming into California. Immigration must stop."
Harold Gilliam, environmental writer, *San Francisco Chronicle*, February 21, 1993.

"Providence has been pleased to give this one connected country, to one united people, a people descended from the same ancestors, speaking the same language,

19

professing the same religion, attached to the same principles of government, very similar in their manners and customs, and who, by their joint counsels, arms and efforts fighting side by side throughout a long and bloody war, have nobly established their general Liberty and Independence."
The Federalist, No. 2. 1787, John Jay.

"We're an immigrant country and we'll continue to be an immigrant country. If we stop taking immigrants, we will fundamentally alter what we are. Our unity is not dependent on uniformity. It's dependent on diversity. If we don't have diversity, we won't have uniformity."
Charles Keely, professor of international migration at Georgetown University, *Minneapolis Star Tribune*, October 8, 1992.

"However one cuts it, the question is not whether there are limits to this country's ability to absorb immigration; the question is only where those limits lie, and how they should be determined and enforced—whether by rational decision at this end or by the ultimate achievement of some sort of a balance of misery between this country and the vast pools of poverty elsewhere that now confront it."
George Kennan, former U.S. Ambassador to the Soviet Union, *Around the Cragged Hill*, 1993.

"...I believe that it is not enough, as I said, to tinker at the margins of U.S. immigration law...the United States must institute comprehensive reforms that conform to the realities of the era in which we live."
Senator Harry Reid, D-Nevada, on the Senate floor on September 20, 1993.

"As a sovereign nation, the United States has a right and a duty to control our borders."
Frank Sharry, *Brokaw Report*, March 28, 1993.

"The purpose of immigration is to create Americans."
Joel Kotkin, author of *Tribes*, *Seattle Post-Intelligencer*, June 19, 1994.

"Give me your tired, your poor, your huddled masses, yearning to breathe free, the wretched refuse of your teeming shore. Send these, the homeless, tempest-tost to me: I lift my lamp beside the golden door."
Emma Lazarus, *The New Colossus.*

"When one considers present immigration policies, it seems we have insensibly reverted to mass immigration, without ever having made a decision to do so. Few Americans believe our population is too low, our land too lightly settled, our resources unexploited, our industries and commerce short of labor. But our policies, the result of various pressures operating within a framework of decent and generous ideals, end up looking as if we believe all this is true."
Nathan Glazer, *The New Republic*, December 27, 1993.

"There's nothing wrong with people deciding who comes and who comes from where. This is our country and I think you've got a right. Somebody's got to decide. Why should it not be those of us who live here, and so that doesn't seem to me to be the least bit unfair."
Pat Buchanan, *BorderLine*, June 11, 1996.

"Immigration into America is not a natural or God-given right. It is something the nation adjusts from time to time as it wishes to suit the national interest."
James O. Goldsborough, columnist, *San Diego Union-Tribune*, June 15, 1995.

"The simple fact is that we must not and we will not surrender our borders to those who wish to exploit our history of compassion and justice."
President Bill Clinton, *New York Times*, July 28, 1993.

The Economic Argument

Well, many people think, if tradition isn't the real reason immigration is so high, it must be economic need—in our country, the economy drives everything. That line of thinking is why we move on now to tackle the common myth that "immigration is necessary (or simply good) for the economy."

This objection is a favorite of hard-core opponents of reform, particularly corporate employers (who like having access to cheap foreign labor) and from ivory-tower economists (who are interested only in the size of the overall economy, not how it affects you). Such opponents have swayed the thinking of many well-intentioned business-boosters, who have taken their assertions about immigration as articles of faith.

But these opponents ignore the fact that what might be "good" or convenient for business is often bad for the public (just think about industrial pollution). While quick to claim that they can make a bigger profit by using immigrants, they shrink from seeing how the costs of immigration are then passed on to the general public—that their private gain is a public loss.

What follows are three examples of approaches to making an economic argument in favor of immigration reform. While you will seldom have the opportunity to go into the detail you will find here, you will find that, in a society as economically-oriented as ours, tackling the economic objection with arguments of your own is always a good idea.

ECONOMIC ARGUMENT NO. 1:
THE COSTS OF IMMIGRATION
OR
WHY IMMIGRATION IS AN ECONOMIC BURDEN

The truth is, most immigrants are poor; indeed, that is why they come here. Through present immigration policy, we are admitting 800,000 to 900,000 mostly poor people in our society every year—a society which is already challenged to deal with the poverty of its natives.

The cost of the immigrants to our society is enormous. The most recent estimate places the costs of post-1969 immigrants at $65 billion in 1996 alone ($40.5 billion from legal immigrants and $24.5 billion from illegal immigrants. This is the net cost; that is, **after** immigrants' contribution in taxes is counted in their favor.

As high as the cost is now, the rising tide of immigration will lift it even higher in years to come. By 2006, the annual net cost of immigration will be $108 billion—66 percent higher than the cost in 1996. The net national cumulative costs for the decade 1997–2006 for all post-1969 immigrants will be $866 billion, an average of almost $87 billion a year.[16]

---

[16]*The Net Costs of Immigration: The Facts, The Trends, and The Critics*, Dr. Donald Huddle, Department of Economics, Rice University, October 22, 1996.

Program	Amounts in Billions[17]		
	Legal	Illegal	Total
Public Education K-12	$14.38	$5.85	$20.23
Public Higher Education	$5.55	$0.71	$6.26
ESL and Bilingual Education	$2.82	$1.22	$4.04
Food Stamps	$2.81	$0.85	$3.66
AFDC	$2.71	$0.50	$3.21
Supplemental Security Income (SSI)	$2.76	———	$2.76
Housing	$2.37	$0.61	$2.98
Social Security	$21.92	$3.61	$25.53
Earned Income Tax Credit	$3.69	$0.68	$4.37
Medicaid	$11.43	$3.12	$14.55
Medicare A and B	$5.49	$0.58	$6.07
Criminal Justice and Corrections	$2.32	$0.76	$3.08
Local Government	$15.32	$5.00	$20.32
Other Programs	$18.41	$9.25	$27.66
Total Costs	$111.98	$32.74	$144.70
Less Taxes Paid	$82.38	$12.59	$94.97
Net Costs of Direct Services	$29.60	$20.16	$49.76
Displacement Costs	$10.96	$4.28	$15.24
All Net Costs	**$40.56**	**$24.44**	**$65.00**
Percent of Net Costs	62.4%	37.6%	100%

Some estimates are even higher. A 1995 study from the National Bureau of Economic Research, based on the Census Bureau's Survey of Income and Program Participation, analyzed immigrants' specific use of means-tested welfare (both direct and indirect), and found that the total immigrant receipt of welfare in 1996 came to $180 billion.[18]   That annual amount is sure to grow as the

---

[17]*The Net Costs of Immigration: The Facts, The Trends, and The Critics*, Dr. Donald Huddle, Department of Economics, Rice University, October 22, 1996.

[18]*Immigration and the Welfare State*, George Borjas and Lynette Hilton, Working Paper Series #5372, National Bureau of Economic Research, December 1995.

$

population of legal and illegal immigrants —now at 25 million—receives over a million new people every year.

All these costs do not even take into account the deficit created by the descendants of post-1969 immigrants, who are estimated to bring the cost to over $100 billion a year.[19] But even this estimate is overly optimistic. With immigration policy skewed toward relatives in underdeveloped countries and away from skilled admissions, the flow of immigrants is increasingly composed of the unskilled and undereducated. As a result, "immigrants arriving in the past decade or so are earning less compared to native-born Americans than immigrants who arrived in earlier decades." In other words, the overall earning power of the immigrant population will continue to deteriorate, making them an even bigger drain on our society.

Occasionally, there have been studies that have claimed to find that immigrants create less of a deficit (or even a surplus). But these studies are marred by common flaws, such as using old data on the immigrants of twenty or thirty years ago and the omission of whole categories of less skilled immigrants in order to fudge the calculations in immigrants' favor.[20]

While the cost of taking care of poor immigrants may be shifted by legislation among the levels of government and the private sector, the fact remains that immigration creates an enormous fiscal burden on America and its citizens—a

---

[19] *Huddle, ibid.*

[20] For example, a 1994 Urban Institute study, *Migration and Immigrants: Setting the Record Straight*, found that immigration created a surplus of $29 billion annually, but only after it excluded from its calculations all immigrants from Mexico, Cambodia, Cuba, Czechoslovakia, Hungary, Poland, the former U.S.S.R., and Vietnam.

$

burden that Congress has levied upon us through short-sighted and haphazard immigration policymaking.

Americans should demand that Congress reduce the immigrant flow and alter the criteria for admission to ameliorate the cost of immigration to our society.

ECONOMIC ARGUMENT NO. 2:
IMMIGRATION AND WAGE DEPRESSION
OR
HOW IMMIGRATION LOWERS AMERICAN WORKERS' WAGES

High-immigration cheerleaders claim that we need immigration for our economy. But they ignore the detrimental effect that importing workers has on American workers, particularly low-skilled natives. In a supply-and-demand economy like ours, the more of something there is, the less value it has. By artificially inflating the number of workers in our country, immigration lowers the value of workers, and wages are depressed. As one expert has noted, "I know business people who tell me they're not interested in hiring Americans because the people who come from outside are cheaper. But ...if there's an unlimited supply of labor facing this country from outside, from the South or wherever, at five dollars an hour, I don't care how fast this economy grows, the wage rate for such people is going to be five dollars an hour!"[21]

Most of the immigrants being admitting are low-skilled. Only 5 percent of immigrants admitted in 1995 were admitted as skilled workers. Out of all the working-age immigrants admitted in 1995, 47 percent had no profession, occupation, or job at all.[22] The average immigrant has only a

---

[21]Robert Dunn, professor of economics at George Washington University, *BorderLine*, NET Televsion, May 29, 1996.

[22]INS Statistics Division, 1996.

ninth-grade education; more than a third of immigrants over 25 are not high school graduates.[23]

Some employers claim that they need to import low-skilled workers to compete in the world market, where wages are very low. But those employers have simply become dependent on cheap foreign labor to the detriment of the American worker: "Network recruitment [of immigrants] not only excludes American workers from certain jobs; it also builds a dependency relationship between U.S. employers and Mexican sources that requires a constant infusion of new workers."[24] Such a strategy for our economy is doomed to failure anyway: "The low-wage strategy may work in the short run, but in the long run it's a loser. In the long run, we are not going to win a wage-cutting contest with the Third World."[25]

Besides, the United States already has plenty of low-skilled native workers: "No technologically advanced industrial nation that has 27 million illiterate adults ... need have any fear about a shortage of unskilled workers in its foreseeable future."[26] In 1996, while there were nearly seven and a half million unemployed American workers, the U.S. admitted over 900,000 immigrants.[27]

---

[23]U.S. Census Bureau, 1995.

[24]"Network Recruitment and Labor Displacement," *Immigration 2000*, Phillip Martin, 1992.

[25]Former U.S. Secretary of Labor Ray Marshall, "Third Rate Workers for a Third World Economy," *New Perspectives Quarterly,* Volume 7, No. 4, Fall 1990.

[26]"Immigration Policy and Work Force Preparedness," Vernon Briggs, *ILR Report*, Vol. 28, No.1, Fall 1990.

[27]Bureau of Labor Statistics Unemployment Division, and the INS Statistics Division.

$

The effect of immigration on those low-skilled Americans is profound, and your government knows it: "Undoubtedly, access to lower-wage foreign workers has a depressing effect [on wages]."[28]   Government research suggests that 50 percent of wage-loss among low-skilled Americans is due to the immigration of low-skilled workers.[29] Some native workers lose not just wages but their jobs through immigrant competition.   An estimated 1,880,000 American workers are displaced from their jobs every year by immigration; the cost for providing welfare and assistance to these Americans is over $15 billion a year.[30]

The effects are most pronounced in the cities where immigrants go. High immigration cities have twice as much unemployment as low immigration cities.[31]   Because too much immigration keeps wages low, wage increases in low-immigration cities have been 48 percent higher than in high-immigration cities.[32] Thus, immigration contributes to the growing disparity between the rich and the poor in this country,[33] and the shrinking of the middle class.[34] But the

---

[28]U.S. Labor Secretary Robert Reich, November 1995.

[29]"Skill Differences and the Effect of Immigrants on the Wages of Natives," Working Paper 273, Bureau of Labor Statistics, December 1995, David Jaeger.

[30]*The Net Costs of Immigration*, Donald Huddle, Rice University, October 1996.

[31]*A Tale of Ten Cities: Immigration's Effect on the Family Environment in American Cities*, Scipio Garling and Leon Bouvier, 1995.

[32]"Linked Migration Systems: Immigration and Internal Labor Flows in the United States," *Economic Geography*, July 1992, Richard Wright.

[33]Annual Report of the Council of Economic Advisors, U.S. GPO, 1994.

[34]*What is the Relationship Between Income Inequality and Immigration?*, John Martin, October 1996.

damage is not confined to high-immigration locales. The harm is carried to other cities when poor Americans whose wages have been depressed or who have been displaced from their jobs by immigration move to low-immigration areas in search of greener pastures.[35]

In short, the mass importation of low-skilled workers through immigration damages the job market for Americans, depresses wages for low-skilled natives, and costs the taxpayer billions a year—all for the benefit of businesses that have become dependent on cheap, foreign labor. An immigration system that admits too many people, without regard to their skill levels or impact on the labor force is to blame. We must reform the immigration laws to lower the level of annual immigration to our country and to ensure that those immigrants who are admitted complement, not compete, with our native labor force.

---

[35]*Immigration and Internal Migration for U.S. States*, William Frey, Population Studies Center, Ann Arbor, Michigan, 1994.

Economic Argument No. 3:
The Truth About the
Employment-Based
Immigration System
or
Why the Wall Street Journal is
Wrong about Immigration

Big business likes to claim that our present high level of immigration—800,000 to 900,000 a year— is necessary for their survival and the robustness of our economy. Arguing on their behalf, George Gilder editorialized in the *Wall Street Journal*:

> *Without immigration, the U.S. would not exist as a world power. ... Today, immigrants are vital not only for targeted military projects but also for the wide range of leading-edge ventures in an information age economy. No less than military superiority in previous eras, U.S. industrial dominance and high standards of living today depend on outsiders.*[36]

Many Americans would find this idea—that American know-how and ingenuity must be imported from abroad—absurd, and a brief look at the facts about what business is actually doing with its part of the immigration system backs up their reaction.

The bulk of immigrants are admitted because they have a relative here—nepotism, in effect. Only a small part of overall annual immigration comes through employment-based admissions (the people admitted as immigrants for

---

[36]"Geniuses From Abroad," *Wall Street Journal*, December 18, 1995.

32

business purposes and at business' demand). In fact, only 12 percent of immigrant admissions in 1995 were in the employment-based category—just 85,336 people.

Big business would have the public think that these 85,000 people were indispensable. But to whom did those employment-based admissions really go? A lot of those 85,000 admissions didn't go to workers at all (employment-based "principals," as they are called); they went to their children and spouses. The actual number of principals—people business might claim to need—was 36,982. But if you think that these principals are all scientists and engineers—the kinds of technological specialists business claims it needs so much—you are wrong. Only 5,066 (a mere 14 percent of the employment-based principals; a scant 6 percent of the total employment-based admissions; and a neglible $^7/_{10}$ of a percent of total immigrant admissions) were engineers, mathematicians, computer scientists, or natural scientists. It seems hard to believe that business couldn't find—or our educational system produce—another 5,000 Americans in those professions if we chose to end our dependence on foreign labor.

So, who are the rest of the 37,000 people that the world's largest economy can't do without, if not hi-tech pioneers?

- 7,305 were in executive, administrative and managerial occupations;
- 6,904 were in service occupations;
- 6,959 were in health occupations;
- 3,962 were various other professions[37]

---

[37]Teachers, counselors, librarians, archivists, curators, social scientists, urban planners, lawyers, writers, artists, entertainers, athletes, salespeople, administrative support, clerical workers, farmers, fishermen, and foresters.

$

- 2,996 were craftsmen, repairmen, operators, and laborers;
- 1,793 were social, recreational, or religious workers;
- 1,235 were technicians; and
- 1,572 had no occupation at all or were "occupation unknown".[38]

It is hard to credit claims by big business that they can't do without aliens in most of these occupations.

Despite what big business claims, it uses very few of the employment visas for the high-tech workers it says it needs—fewer every year, in fact.

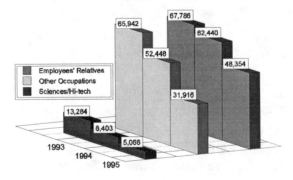

Few Employment Admissions Used
for Hi-Tech Immigrants

---

[38]INS Statistics Division.

Other Quotes About Economics

"Low-skilled jobs are disappearing in this country. You've got attrition of unskilled jobs occurring at the same time you've got a lot of unskilled workers ... and those people are not going to go away. There's no excuse for bringing immigrants, illegal or otherwise, into such a labor market."
Vernon Briggs, Cornell University economist, *BorderLine*, April 11, 1996.

"I know business people who tell me they're not interested in hiring Americans because the people who come from outside are cheaper. But if one is interested in the increased inequity of income — if there's an unlimited supply of labor facing this country from outside, from the South or wherever, at five dollars an hour, I don't care how fast this economy grows, the wage rate for such people is going to be five dollars an hour!"
Robert Dunn, professor of economics at George Washington University, *BorderLine*, May 29, 1996.

"In fiscal costs, the cost to the government was $29 billion negative for immigration. This is all immigrants, legal as well as illegal. In other words. $29 billion more was spent by the government than was received in taxes. ... What is $29 billion? It's about 14 million personal computers that could have been sent to schools and poor school districts. It's equivalent to the entire gross domestic product of Mexico, interestingly enough. It's equivalent to the entire railroad industry. ...And interestingly, it's more than all federal

spending on the Justice Department, the State Department and the Interior Department combined."
Mark Krikorian, executive director of the Center for Immigration Studies, *BorderLine*, April 17, 1996.

"We have looked for, and have not found, any convincing economic arguments for continued national population growth. The health of the economy does not depend on it. The vitality of business does not depend on it."
President's Commission on Population Growth and the American Future, 1972.

"...It appears that [immigrants] may have slowed the growth-rate of native workers' earnings, with a disproportionate effect on low-skill occupations. Immigration had the largest wage dampening effects on immigrants themselves. Their wage rates grew twice as slowly as other workers' rates."
George Vernez and David Ronfeldt, The Rand Corporation, *Science Magazine*, March 8, 1991.

"We should strengthen our immigration laws to prevent the importation of foreign wages and working conditions. We should make it illegal for employers to lay off Americans and then fill their jobs by bringing in workers from overseas. Any U.S. employer who wishes to hire from abroad —even for temporary jobs—should have to recruit U.S. workers first. And we should end the unskilled immigration that competes with young Americans just entering the job market."
Senator Ted Kennedy, February 8, 1996, speech to the Center for National Policy.

"Our immigration must be more finely tuned than in the past if they [immigrants] are to ease and not complicate the impending changes in our labor force and occupational profile. Those policies must discourage the flow of foreign workers into low-skilled declining occupations, while meeting the needs for higher education and training of Americans and earlier waves of immigrants."
Malcolm Lovell, Jr., Director of Institute for Labor and Management at The George Washington University testifying before the Senate Immigration Subcommittee on the Kennedy-Simpson immigration bill, March 15, 1990.

"It is obviously easier, for the short run, to draw cheap labor from adjacent pools of poverty...than to find it among one's own people. And to the millions of such prospective immigrants from poverty to prosperity, there is, rightly or wrongly, no place that looks more attractive than the United States. Given its head, and subject to no restrictions, this pressure will find its termination only when the levels of overpopulation and poverty in the United States are equal to those of the countries from which these people are now so anxious to escape."
George F. Kennan, *Around the Cragged Hill*, 1993.

"Actually, the inability of any society to resist immigration, the inability to find other solutions to the problem of employment at the lower, more physical, and menial levels of the economic process, is a serious weakness, and possibly even a fatal one, in any national society. The fully healthy society would find ways to meet those needs out of its own resources."
George F. Kennan, *Around the Cragged Hill*, 1993.

$

"The immigration law is a burden to our economy. These men do jobs no one else will do. A city like Los Angeles needs slave labor —that's the only way to put it." Rev. Michael E. Kennedy of Our Lady Queen of Angels Roman Catholic Church in Los Angeles, FAIR *Immigration Report*, October 1988, explaining why his church was giving sanctuary to illegal aliens.

"If real wages of poorer Americans are to increase and the inequality of incomes is to be reduced, there must be some restriction on the foreign supply of low-wage labor, and that means both stricter immigration policies and tougher enforcement measures." Robert Dunn, Jr., *Washington Post*, August 25, 1992.

"We can't afford to lose control of our own borders or to take on new financial burdens at a time when we are not adequately providing for the jobs, the health care and the education of our own people." President Bill Clinton, *Washington Times*, June 20, 1994.

"It would be a much better policy to have the Labor Dept. recruit U.S. citizens available for work. If the Government can locate enough U.S. workers for a given harvest, the growers should be prohibited from hiring aliens for the job. Unless the Labor Dept. curbs these kinds of abuses, it will contribute to the poverty of thousands of American farm workers." Ray Marshall, Secretary of Labor under President Jimmy Carter and professor of economics and public affairs at University of Texas, *New York Times*, August 25, 1993.

$

"The shortages we are experiencing are not shortages in absolute numbers. They are shortages of properly trained people in various places for particular kinds of jobs, and they can be overcome by aggressive public and private investment in human capital improvements."
Interface, Department of Professional Employees, AFL-CIO Summer 1990.

"The new immigrants are joining welfare at a much higher rate than the older immigrants. It's a net loss for the country. They're taking more out of the country than they're putting in. They seem to be more unskilled and they have less education."
George J. Borjas, University of California at San Diego, *New York Times*, December 3, 1991.

"The fact that immigrants reside in a relatively small number of localities also magnifies the group's impact on the native labor market. Due to their extreme geographic concentration, a ten percent increase in the size of the immigration flow amounts to a doubling of the immigration population in a small number of cities. This major increase in the number of foreign workers entering the local labor market could have a significant adverse effect on the earnings and employment opportunities of natives. Moreover, the geographic concentration of immigrants may cause significant strains in the provision of social services and bloat the welfare budgets of affected areas. This is particularly true of large and unexpected refugee flows into certain metropolitan areas, such as the 1980 Mariel boatlift into Miami or even larger influx of Southeast Asian refugees into a few California cities. For example, a study of settlement patterns of Indochinese refugees reported that more than ninty percent of refugees initially resettled into San Diego and San Francisco have been applying for public assistance within weeks after their arrival in the U.S."

George Borjas, author of *Friends or Strangers, The Impact of Immigration on the U.S. Economy.*

$

The Social Argument

As important as the economy is, it is part of something much larger—our entire society. The social arguments for immigration reform address the broader effects of immigration on our society. Much of the "cost" of immigration that is passed on to the public is not simply a tax bill, but is a deterioration of our quality of life.

Overburdening the educational system, endangering public health, worsening our crime problem, squeezing out native minorities, increasing ethnic tension, widening the language gap—immigration policy's effects on our society are manyfold.

Many citizens — including some immigration reformers — have difficulty confronting some of these effects. They worry that to bring them up is to accuse immigrants themselves, to somehow condemn them as *bad.* That feeling, while understandable, is misplaced. Judging the results of immigration policy is not the same as judging immigrants personally. And what better moral ground for judging public policy could there be than judging its effects on society?

What follows are three examples of social arguments in favor of immigration reform. While you will seldom have the opportunity to go into the detail you will find here, you should use the social argument every time you discuss the issue. Many citizens who may turn a deaf ear to history and economics will listen carefully when you begin to discuss the daily impact of immigration on the society they live in.

SOCIAL ARGUMENT NO. 1:
IMMIGRATION AND BLACK
AMERICANS
OR
WHY BLACK AMERICANS SUPPORT
IMMIGRATION REFORM

"To review the Black side of our nation's
immigration tradition is to observe African
Americans periodically trying to climb the
mainstream economic ladder, only to be
shoved aside each time. It is to see one
immigrant wave after another climb onto and
up that ladder while planting their feet on the
backs of Black Americans. ... The most racist
policy in this country for the past 25 years has
been our immigration policy because it has
been the worst thing that has happened to the
Blacks from the federal government since
slavery."
Roy Beck, *The Case Against Immigration*, 1996.

One of the cruelest effects of high-level immigration
to the U.S. is its worsening of the plight of black Americans.

Historically, blacks have suffered as a result of
immigration. In the first half of the 1800s, immigration
blocked blacks from opportunities for economic mobility in
the United States. Frederick Douglass was moved to say,
"The old employments by which we have heretofore gained
our livelihood, are gradually, and it may seem inevitably,
passing into other hands. Every hour sees the black man
elbowed out of employment by some newly arrived immigrant

42

whose hunger and whose color are thought to give him a better title to the place." During the post-Civil War industrial expansion, blacks were shunted aside from entry level positions by business owners who preferred to hire white immigrants, who were then brought in *en masse*. By 1896, the unfairness of the situation was so stark that Booker T. Washington pleaded:

> "To those of the white race who look to the incoming of those of foreign birth and strange tongue and habits, [I say] cast down your bucket where you are. Cast it down among the eight millions of Negroes ... who shall stand by you with a devotion no foreigner can approach, ready to lay down their lives, if need be, in defense of yours, interlacing our industrial, commercial, civil, and religious life with yours in a way that shall make the interests on both races one."

The situation today is similar. During the Civil Rights era of the 1950s and 1960s, which was to have "freed" black Americans socially and economically, Congress also changed immigration law to allow close to a million immigrants a year—to compete with blacks for entry level positions.

According to recent studies, immigrants displace a disproportionate number of black workers and lower their wages. For example, a GAO study found that a decade of heavy immigration to Los Angeles had changed the janitorial industry from a mostly unionized native black workforce to one of non-unionized immigrants. According to the Census, the employment of black Americans as hotel workers in California dropped 30 percent in the 1980s, while the number of immigrants with such jobs rose 166 percent. A similar story can be told of the garment industry, the restaurant business, hospital work, and public service jobs. The Bureau of Labor Statistics found in a recent study that immigration accounts for about 50 percent of the decline in real wages for

43

the lowest-skilled American workers, many of whom are blacks.

Immigration has also undermined the attempts of "Affirmative Action" to help advance black Americans. George LaNoue, professor of political science at the University of Maryland, points out, "Affirmative action that was originally designed to compensate for the decades of discrimination against American blacks has been turned into a system where many of the beneficiaries, and in some environments, some cities, some sectors, **most** of the beneficiaries are people of fairly recent immigrant origin."

Black Americans are aware of immigration's impact and generally support immigration reform. The Roper Organization found in 1995 that 72 percent of black Americans think that immigration should be cut to less than a third of its present level. Gerri Williams, editor of *Immigration Impact: Documenting the Effects of Immigration on African Americans*, has noted, "as with earlier waves of immigration, African Americans have experienced the effects of this influx first and hardest. In education, politics, the labor market, social services, and more, the pressures caused by record levels of immigration are being felt in the black community. Immigration is one of the most significant forces affecting African Americans today."

While immigration reform would not be a panacea for all the difficulties of black Americans, it is obviously a step in the right direction. Congress must recognize that its policy of excessive immigration creates more obstacles to black advancement and should reduce admissions immediately.

Social Argument No. 2:
How Immigration Threatens the Future for American Youth
or
Why Parents Should Support Immigration Reform

Many people who support present immigration policy seem to do so with no regard for how it threatens the future of American youth.

Immigrants are overwhelming school systems. Schools are already overcrowded; there are six million more children in school now than 10 years ago. By 2002, the school population will grow from 49 million to 55 million—because of immigration.[39] Without school-age immigrants (about 250,000 a year) and the children of immigrants (about 725,000 a year), school enrollment would not be rising at all.[40] The estimated cost to the American taxpayer for the education of immigrants' children is over $30 billion a year.[41]

Foreign students are taking the place of American undergraduates in our colleges. There are over 452,000 foreign students in American colleges. Between 1988 and 1992, alien college students received $1.8 billion in federal

---

[39]The National Center for Educational Statistics.

[40]The Center for Immigration Studies.

[41]*The Net Costs of Immigration: The Facts, The Trends, and The Critics*, Donald Huddle, October 22, 1996.

Pell grants for higher education. All of this money might have gone to aid the education of American citizens.

It is projected that our economy will create 22 million new jobs over the next ten years. During that same time, 17 million people from our present population—most of them new graduates—will enter the workforce.[42]

This sounds like a formula for success: a tighter labor market, more available jobs for the young, better wages and working conditions. But during that same period, 6.5 million immigrants are expected to enter the job market, canceling out any effects of that job creation.[43] The result: continued unemployment and underemployment, stagnant wages for workers, particularly entry level ones like recent graduates.

Even high-skilled graduates are not immune. Foreign students are also taking the place of American graduate students and Ph.D.s. These foreign students are particularly attractive to universities and employers when they can use them to accomplish Affirmative Action goals.

As a result, there is a glut of science Ph.D.s coming out of our graduate schools (about 22 percent more than are needed); more than a third of them are foreign students, an estimated 50 percent of whom remain in the country after getting their degrees.[44] By flooding the job market, they depress working wages for all "post-docs".

The employment-based visa system also increases competition for our young adults. Of the immigrants admitted under this system, around sixty percent are not specialists brought to fill holes in our workforce; they are

---

[42]Bureau of Labor Statistics.

[43]INS Statistics Division.

[44] "The Future of the Ph.D.", *Science*, October 6, 1995.

young people with college degrees who compete with our own young for professional positions.[45]

Most immigrants are not specialists or Ph.D.s, but rather are low-skilled and undereducated. The median education level for adult immigrants is less than a ninth grade education[46]; and high-immigration cities have sixty percent more drop-outs than low-immigration cities.[47] These immigrants compete for jobs with the least skilled of our citizens, our young.

The bussing, gardening, babysitting, hotel work, housecleaning, waitering, and delivery that used to be done by teenagers and collegians is now dominated by recent immigrants. The glut of workers available for low-skill jobs caused by immigration has kept down the wages and conditions of those jobs. For example, an estimated fifty percent of wage depression among high-school dropouts is attributable to competition from immigrants.[48]

The threat is not just an immediate economic one, but a long-term environmental one as well. Immigration is the engine of runaway population growth in this country, making the U.S. one of the few developed nations that is not stabilizing its population. 52 percent of our population

---

[45]INS Statistics Division.

[46]The Center for Educational Statistics.

[47]*A Tale of Ten Cities: Immigration's Effect on the Family Environment in American Cities*, Scipio Garling and Leon Bouvier, 1995.

[48]*Skill Differences and the Effect of Immigrants on the Wages of Natives*, Working Paper 273, Bureau of Labor Statistics, December 1995.

growth since 1970 has been due to immigration[49], as has been 48 percent of the increase in U.S. use of energy.[50]

America's teenagers are aware of the threat. When *Who's Who Among American High School Students* surveyed 8000 students aged 16–18, 59 percent of the respondents said that immigration policies will make it harder for them to get the job they want, and 52 percent said the U.S. has too many immigrants.[51] The National Association of Secondary School Principals' comprehensive study of the attitudes of American teenagers found that 67 percent of students aged 13–17 think that legal immigration to the US should be reduced.[52] Our government should take seriously the concerns of our young for their future and bring a halt to most forms of legal immigration.

---

[49]The U.S.Census Bureau, and *Re-Charting America's Future*, Roy Beck, 1994.

[50]"The Consequences of Rapid Population Growth in the United States are Staggering," Population-Environment Balance, November 9, 1996; "Population and the Energy Problem," *Population and Environment*, Spring 1991, John Holdren.

[51]"Teens Say There Are Too Many Immigrants," Associated Press, November 11, 1996.

[52]*The Mood of American Youth 1996*, The Horatio Alger Association of Distinguished Americans and the National Association of Secondary School Principals.

Social Argument No. 3:
Immigrants and Public Health
or
Why Immigration is a
Health Care Problem

While many of the effects of heavy immigration are well known (such as the depression of American wages, strain on the educational system, and the potential for ethnic strife), the impact on our public health of admitting around one million people from countries with less developed health care is often overlooked.

Immigrants are vastly underinsured. Forty-three percent of noncitizens under 65 have no health insurance. That means there are 6.2 million uninsured immigrants, who constitute 15 percent of the total uninsured in the nation.[53] In fact, attempts by Immigration and Naturalization Service officers to check whether immigrants have health insurance have been quashed by the INS management.[54] The cost of the

---

[53]Employee Benefit Research Group study, January 1995. "The study suggests the very high degree to which that population is contributing to uncompensated costs. " EBRI President Dallas Salisbury, *Washington Post*, January 25, 1995.

[54]"Over the years, Adjudications Officers ... have requested that [applicants] provide evidence that they have comprehensive medical health insurance prior to granting these applicants lawful permanent residence. These requests have been made ostensibly to ensure that the applicant does not become a public charge by accessing the health care system in the public sector ... [However,] there is no regulatory requirement that applicants for lawful permanent residence obtain medical health insurance as a prerequisite to receiving lawful permanent residence. ... Therefore, all Adjudications Officers will discontinue the

medical care of these uninsured immigrants is passed onto the taxpayer, and strains the financial stability of the health care community.

Another problem is immigrants' use of hospital and emergency services rather than preventative medical care. For example, the utilization rate of hospitals and clinics by illegal aliens (29 percent) is more than twice that of the total U.S. population (11 percent).[55]

As a result, the costs of medical care for immigrants are staggering. The annual bill to the taxpayers for Medicaid given to immigrants is over $14 billion ($11.4 billion to legal immigrants, and $3.1 billion to illegal aliens). The cost is compounded by the immigrant bill for Medicare, $6.1 billion a year ($5.5 billion to legal immigrants and $.6 billion to illegal aliens).

As serious as these problems are, they are dwarfed by the threat of reintroducing serious contagious diseases into our society. "Contagious diseases that are generally considered to have been controlled in the United States are readily evident along the border. ... The incidence of tuberculosis in El Paso County is twice that of the U.S. rate[.] [Director of the El Paso heath district] Dr. Laurence Nickey also reports that leprosy, which is considered by most Americans to be a disease of the Third World, is readily evident along the U.S.-Mexico border and that dysentery is several times the U.S. rate. ... People have come to the border for economic opportunities[,] but the necessary sewage

---

practice of routinely requiring medical health insurance for ... applicants." Steven Farquharson, INS Office of Examinations, memo, April 1, 1994.

[55] *Assessment of Potential Impact of Undocumented Person on National Health Reform*, National Health Foundation, April 14, 1993.

treatment facilities, public water systems, environmental enforcement[,] and medical care have not been made available to them, causing a severe risk to health and well being of people on both sides of the border."[56]

"The pork tapeworm, which thrives in Latin America and Mexico, is showing up along the U.S. border, threatening to ravage victims with symptoms ranging from seizures to death. ... The same [Mexican] underclass has migrated north to find jobs on the border, bringing the parasite and the sickness—cysticercosis—its eggs can cause[.] Cysts that form around the larvae usually lodge in the brain and destroy tissue, causing hallucinations, speech and vision problems, severe headaches, strokes, epileptic seizures, and in rare cases death."[57]

Typhoid struck Silver Spring, Maryland, in 1992 when an immigrant from the Third World, (who had been working in food service in the United States for almost two years) transmitted the bacteria through food at the McDonald's where she worked. River blindness, malaria, guinea worm, have all been brought to Northern Virginia by immigration.[58]

Contrary to common belief, tuberculosis (TB) has not been wiped out in the United States, mostly due to migration. In 1995, there was an outbreak of TB in an Alexandria high school, when 36 highschoolers caught the disease from an

---

[56]Statement of the American Medical Association to the Committee on Public Works and Transportation, U.S. House of Representatives, May 7, 1991.

[57] *Houston Chronicle*, November 3, 1992.

[58]"Influx of exotic diseases keep doctors hopping," *Fairfax Journal*, May 8, 1992.

51

immigrant student.[59] The four immigrant magnet states have over half the TB cases in the U.S.[60] In 1992, 27 percent of the TB cases in the United States were among the foreign-born; in California, it was 61 percent of the cases; in Hawaii, 83 percent; and in Washington state, 46 percent.

Disease within the immigrant community can be particularly difficult to combat. "Immigrants present a special challenge, as health officials struggle with language and cultural barriers to find active TB cases and cure them before they spread to the general population."[61] "When the migrants develop TB they often remain untreated, as health systems tend to overlook mobile individuals. They can then spread TB to others in crowded housing and can infect otherwise healthy populations as they move through new towns and countries. ... And as many as half the world's refugees my be infected with TB."[62]

Despite the potential danger for public health, there are only eight diseases that bar immigrants from admission.[63] At the current rate at which immigrants are being admitted (between 800,000 and 1,000,000 every year), our government cannot assure that all precautions have been taken to protect

---

[59]"Health officials say there is a correlation between increases in tuberculosis cases in recent years and the influx of residents from countries where disease prevention is substandard." "36 Students in Alexandria Test Positive for TB Exposure," *Washington Post*, June 8, 1995.

[60]"Taking it to the Streets, " *Los Angeles Times*, October 2, 1993.

[61]"Deadly Tuberculosis on the Rise," *Saginaw News*, November 6, 1993.

[62]WHO Report on Tuberculosis, 1996.

[63]Specifically: chancroid, gonorrhea, granuloma inguinale, tuberculosis, leprosy, lymphogranuloma venereum, syphilis, HIV. 42 Code of Federal Regulations Section 34.2(b).

the public well-being. And, of course, illegal immigrants are not screened at all. To better ensure public safety, we must end illegal immigration and slow legal immigration down to manageable levels.

Other Quotes on Social Aspects

"We are Americanizing them [immigrants]; we are getting them to like welfare. Maybe we need to rethink welfare as a pulling mechanism into this country."
Eloise Anderson, California state director of social services, *Seattle Post-Intelligencer*, June 1, 1994.

"Pete Wilson and the pro–Proposition 187 forces have done us a favor by getting young people active and involved in an issue. Hispanics will replace whites, currently the largest group of California's 32 million people, as the largest segment of the population sometime shortly after the turn of the century. They won't forget this."
U.S. Rep. Xavier Becerra, "U.S. Information", November 14, 1994.

"Imagine this: You arrive home after a long day's work, and you find a strange man sitting in your living room, watching your television, eating your popcorn, drinking your beer. He's unarmed and his behavior is not threatening. He says he wants to live in your home and share your bounty until he finds a good job, but he has no money to give you for room and board. Oh, by the way, his wife and two kids will join him in a few weeks, and he wants you to take care of them, too. He seems pleasant enough, but he doesn't say what will happen if you refuse to let him have what he wants. What do you do?"
Ken Bashford, "U.S.Information", November 14, 1994.

"Affirmative action that was originally designed to compensate for the decades of discrimination against

American blacks has been turned into a system where many of the beneficiaries, and in some environments, some cities, some sectors, most of the beneficiaries are people of fairly recent immigrant origin."
George LaNoue, professor of political science at the University of Maryland at Baltimore, *BorderLine*, February 20, 1996.

"The multi-ethnic factor in governance and politics in big urban centers is going to be the central issue for the future, and one that we are unprepared to deal with. The difficulty of talking across cultures and across languages and across traditions—the kinds of things that have divided nation-states for centuries —are to some degree being miniaturized within our cities."
Richard Weinstein, UCLA.

"The most racist policy in this country for the past 25 years has been our immigration policy because it has been the worst thing that has happened to the Blacks from the federal government since slavery. What it has done is, it's filled the labor pools. And unfortunately, there's still a level of racism in this country so people will hire immigrants far ahead of Blacks."
Roy Beck, author of *Re-Charting America's Future*, on *BorderLine*, February 15, 1996.

"The frustrations have been festering for 12 years because federal policy has forced immigration into this area with no programs to accommodate this trust and no dollars for

education or jobs or social services...we have become a repository but no beneficiary of federal actions."
Washington D.C. Mayor Sharon Pratt Kelly, 1991, Testimony to U.S. Civil Rights Commission on D.C. rioting.

"The actions of these three clowns [Senator Dianne Feinstein, Barbara Boxer, and California Governor Pete Wilson] are to be considered very immature and frankly stupid.... They're selling *La Raza* down the river.... For one thing, relations between the white populace and the rest of the community are already bad enough without these so-called leaders fanning the fires of racism.... We were here first and we will be here long after these racists. The Mexican-U.S. connection cannot be stopped. Politicians should know that we are here to stay and at one point in history we will be in power. How you treat us now will determine how we'll treat you once the roles are reversed."
Marcos Gutierrez, *La Oferta Review*, August 25, 1993.

"The more politicians pretend that humanitarianism for immigrants is the only issue, and that U.S. citizens do not suffer from the added competition for jobs, social services and affordable housing, the greater the frustration will be among U.S. workers and taxpayers."
Richard Estrada, *Dallas Morning News*, February 16, 1990.

"Though hardly all Mexican-Americans welcome new arrivals, Mexican-American leaders covet newcomers because they replenish their political base. Mexico is the largest country of emigration on earth. It comes as no real surprise that African-Americans, confronting their own pending displacement as America's largest minority group, rue the

extension of their own hard-won affirmative action gains to just-arrived non-citizens clogging the ranks of the unskilled in a society with ever less need of them."
Richard Estrada, *Wall Street Journal*, November 24, 1993.

"It is the numbers that are proving problematic, not the Hispanic-ness (or the Asian-ness) of the new immigration...if francophone Quebec can bring the Canadian confederation to the brink of disintegration even though France lies an entire ocean away, should there not at least arise a certain reflectiveness about our Southwest, which lies contiguous to an overpopulated Third World nation?"
Carrying Capacity Network, *Focus*, Vol.2, No. 3, 1992, p.27.

"Every year, the population of Southern California grows by 350,000. That's like adding a city the size of Cleveland to our region every year. How are we going to accommodate these people?"
Carl Boronkay, General Manager of the Los Angeles Metropolitan Water District, *Insight*, January 14, 1991.

"Current U.S. immigration policy helps impede assimilation, promote tribalist politics, prolong labor intensive-ness, and undermine productivity and competitiveness."
Chronicles, July 1991.

"...The Hispanic population has increased by as many as 5 million people in the last decade alone. As lawmakers continue to debate the advisability of raising levels of legal immigration, they should ask themselves if it is truly in the interest of U.S. Hispanics and the nation as a whole to import

more impoverished immigrants at a time when increasing
numbers of U.S. Hispanics find themselves slipping down the
socioeconomic ladder, instead of ascending it."
Dallas Morning News, editorial, September 22, 1990.

"The ethnic and cultural composition of America is
changing profoundly. By the year 2010, one out of every five
Americans is likely to be of Hispanic origin, one of African
or Asian origin and three of European. By 2050 the ratios are
likely to be two, one, and two respectively. In other words the
European component will drop from 60 percent to about 40
percent. This will be a very different America from the
largely European America of the recent past, one more likely
to mirror the cultural and philosophical cleavages that already
divide the world. The transformation of America from a
society dominated — and shaped — by a white Anglo-Saxon
Protestant culture into a global mosaic inevitably will involve
a profound shift in values and perhaps some further loss of
social cohesion. ...It is also likely to be disruptive, even
potentially divisive, especially if in the process the unifying
function of a common language and of an inculcated common
political philosophy are deliberately down-graded. A shared
language and a shared constitutional commitment produce the
common foundation on which a nation's cultural consensus
rests, and without them cultural diversity could become
incapable of sustaining social tolerance. The American
society could then face the threat of disintegration." "Out of
Control", Zbigniew Brzezinski.

THE POPULATION-ENVIRONMENT ARGUMENT

Many people resist all the arguments discussed above: they think that tradition is irrelevant, economics is a minor or isolated problem, and social impacts can be best handled by integrating immigrants into society. Not so easy to dismiss are the next set of arguments on population and the environment.

Without immigration, the United States would be well on its way to having a stable population—the key to controlling damage to the environment. With a stable population level, our society could focus on improving our country's quality of life, not just its quantity.

But recent immigration ensures that that will not happen. Our population will spiral upward, as there is less and less of the good life for more and more people, and as we race closer to destroying our country's environment.

Science has shown that, in any species, populations that do not level off meet with disaster. Many citizens who can dismiss social problems with platitudes will find it harder to ignore the hard numbers of population growth and the threat to the environment.

POPULATION-ENVIRONMENT
ARGUMENT No. 1:
MORE IS NOT NECESSARILY
BETTER
OR
WHY POPULATION GROWTH THROUGH
IMMIGRATION IS NOT WISE

Immigration is responsible for 50 percent of the population growth in this country. Why should that concern us—isn't growth good? In fact, growth is not intrinsically good or bad; what matters is how much. The human body serves as an excellent metaphor for human society in this respect. Normal growth, the stable production of new cells at the right rate to replace old ones, is healthy. Runaway growth, the creation of new cells that are not needed and that damage the environment for all cells, is not healthy—we call it cancer.

The United States has already passed the point where "growth is good." In a report in 1972, an ambitious two-year study by a joint presidential-congressional commission, which had representatives of major corporations and unions, governments, environmental organizations, and urban, ethnic, and women's groups, concluded: "We have looked for, and have not found, any convincing economic argument for continued population growth. The health of our country does not depend on it, nor does the vitality of business nor the welfare of the average person."[64] At the time, the population

---

[64]Report of the Commission on Population Growth and the American Future, 1972.

was only 205 million; now the population is over 266 million—30 percent higher than when the commission saw no need for growth.

One reason for the belief in the necessity of growth is that larger cities originally were formed so that industries there could gain advantages in production. But the technological advances of a shrinking world have rendered many of those advantages neglible. Now we see that the building up large concentrations of population in a city creates disadvantages of scale: increased costs, traffic congestion, pollution. Neither does military superiority equate with a large population as it did in centuries past. As the Gulf War demonstrated, the number of soldiers is relatively meaningless compared to their training and the quality of military technology.

The problems of increased growth have become obvious. 1.3 million acres (an area the size of Delaware) are being blacktopped each year.[65] Current projections suggest a tripling of traffic congestion by the year 2005.[66] Most Americans already live at population densities that are among the highest on earth.[67] Such truths point out that: "Continuous growth is impossible. We must understand that

---

[65]"Land, Energy, and Water: The Constraints Governing Ideal U.S. Population Size", David Pimentel, *Elephants in the Volkswagen*, Lindsey Grant ed., 1992.

[66]*Ice Melter Newsletter*, May 1992.

[67]*Crowding Out the Future*, Robert Fox and Ira Mehlman, 1992.

growth can only be a temporary phenomenon to be followed by stability or decline."[68]

Why must immigration be reduced to achieve a stable population? Because American natives achieved "replacement" rate (a birth-death rate where one child is born for each person dying off) in the 1970s, and would be well on our way to stabilizing the population were it not for one thing: immigration.

At the same time, America's new immigration policies caused the admission of newcomers to skyrocket; in 1996, we admitted more than twice as many immigrants as in 1972, the year of the commission's report. Immigration is increasingly identified as the primary factor to be dealt with in population growth: "Population policy is being made quite incidentally as a by-product of immigration policy. ... [To a large degree, immigration policy **is** population policy, even if it is accidental."[69]

In a country of 266 million people, it may seem that immigration of a million a year is a drop in the bucket. But the real indicator is immigration's share of population growth, which is now 50 percent. Since 1970 our population has grown by about 62 million people. About 30 million of that growth—48 percent—came from immigrants and their descendants.

---

[68]"Discounting the Future", *The Social Contract*, Herbert Woodward, Fall 1991.

[69]*Sobering News from the Real World*, Lindsey Grant, 1995.

U.S. Population Growth, 2000–2050

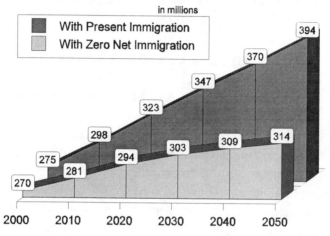

in millions

■ With Present Immigration
□ With Zero Net Immigration

394
370
347
323
298
275
281
294
303
309
314
270

2000   2010   2020   2030   2040   2050

At present, our population is growing by about 2 million people a year; yet legal and illegal immigration are adding about 1.1 people a year—about 55 percent.

If we do not lower the level of immigration back to traditional levels right away, this nation's population will grow to 400 million in the next fifty years. Of that additional 130 million people, 80 million of them—62 percent—will be post-1995 immigrants and their descendants.

Unless you want your children to have to live with 50 percent more people than you live with now—and with the urban expansion, social tension, environmental degradation, and living congestion that extra population will create—you should support immigration reform.

Population-Environment Argument No. 2: Immigration Versus the Environment
or
Why Immigration Reform is Essential to Stopping Environmental Degradation

Since the environmental movement began in the 1960s, Americans have made great strides in reducing their personal impact on the environment.   Practices like carpooling and recycling have become a normal part of our lives, and our industry and governments strive to clean up waste and reduce pollution.   But as a country, our overall damage to the environment has gotten much worse in the last thirty years; all our efforts at conservation are washed away by our steadily increasing population.

Even if the average environmental impact of every American had been reduced 25 percent since 1969 (a feat far beyond the hopes of the most optimistic environmentalists), our country would still be suffering greater damage to our environment, simply because our population has grown 32 percent since then.   After establishing a commission to address the danger of population growth in this country in 1969, President Richard Nixon said, "One of the most serious challenges to human destiny in the last third of this century will be the growth of population.   Whether man's response to that challenge will be a cause for pride or despair in the year 2000 will depend very much on what we do today."

No amount or kind of conservation efforts can succeed if population does not level off; Americans need to stabilize their population to control their environmental degradation. As the environmentalist Izaak Walton League has commented, "Conservationists cannot succeed in protecting our natural heritage unless population becomes part of the solution. Keep the human population level in balance with the limits of nature's renewable resources, or face the eradication of a way of life."

The key to stabilizing the population is arriving at a "replacement rate," that is, a balance between the number of people being born and the number of people dying. In fact, Americans did achieve "replacement rate" in the early 1970s. Yet our population has not leveled off, and isn't going to begin to level off for even the next fifty years. Why? Because of immigration.

President John F. Kennedy wisely pointed out in his book, *A Nation of Immigrants*, "There is, of course, a legitimate argument for some limitation upon immigration. We no longer need settlers for virgin lands, and our economy is expanding more slowly than in the nineteenth and early twentieth century[.]" Yet we have not reduced immigration since then; quite the opposite. Annual immigration is three times what it was in Kennedy's day. And since Nixon's warning in 1969, the U.S. population has grown by about 62 million people—30 million of whom were new immigrants and their descendants. Every year, the U.S. population grows by 2 million people—about 1 million of whom are immigrants.[70]

---

[70] *Re-Charting America's Future*, Roy Beck, 1995.

By 2050, the U.S. population will have grown by another 130 million people—80 million of whom will be post-1995 immigrants and their descendants. Even if all immigration were stopped today, momentum would cause the U.S. population to continue to grow for another 55 years.[71] Yet the government has done nothing to change the immigration policy fueling this population growth, despite the fact that 76 percent of Americans feel that overpopulation is a serious threat to their children and grandchildren in the next twenty-five years.[72] High-population immigration laws stay in place, even though: "It is possible that we have already exceeded our ability to sustain ourselves: estimates of the population we can support, without damaging resource for the next generation, range [up to] 170 million. We are well beyond those limits."[73]

In order to control our damage to the environment, we must stabilize our population, which we cannot do with immigration at its current level. For the sake of our environment, we must greatly reduce average annual immigration and eliminate illegal immigration.

---

[71] *Population Projections*, Bureau of the Census, February 1996.

[72] *Sustainable Development: The New American Dream*, Roper/Starch, March 1996.

[73] Audubon Society, July 1994.

POPULATION-ENVIRONMENT ARGUMENT No. 3: HOW IMMIGRATION HARMS THE SENDING COUNTRIES
OR
DOING HARM BY "DOING GOOD"

Some people think of immigration as a moral obligation of our country; that admitting immigrants to our country shows our concern for the less advantaged and our commitment to helping others. But a brief look at the situation demonstrates that allowing mass immigration as we do now is a poor way of helping others. In fact, it probably does more harm than good.

Brain Drain. The term "brain drain" was first applied to the flight of highly skilled technicians from the war-torn countries of

> "Not only are the developing countries losing some of their most talented citizens, they are also losing the scarce capital that has gone into their rearing and training. Education is, after all, an investment in the future. In the case of brain drain from the developing countries, not only does the investment pay no dividends, but the very capital disappears. Moreover, the exodus of highly skilled professionals deprives the sending countries of the services of the persons on whom campaigns of economic and social development must be based."
> John Tanton, *The Brain Drain and Countries of Emigration*, 1979.

> "The principal loss from prolonged work abroad is the fact that the professional is not contributing to the development of his own country. Instead, he is helping the rich get richer, thereby accentuating inequality among societies. The home country loses its investment in his upbringing and education before he left."
> William Glaser, "International Flows of Talent", *Sourcebook on the New Immigration*, 1980.

Europe to America after World War II, but in recent years the major flow of qualified professionals — physicians, engineers, scientists, educators — has been from the less-developed countries to the more-developed countries. Foreign students account for more than a third of our science Ph.D. students; an estimated 50 percent of them remain in the United States instead of returning to their homelands. In the 1990s, only 15 percent of the immigrants admitted as skilled professionals were from the developed countries of Europe; the rest were from less developed areas like Africa and Asia.

Dissident Drain. In any society, change begins with people who are unhappy with the way things are. The democratization of the Soviet Union was brought about by those who were dissatisfied with its regime. Because of our expansionist i m m i g r a t i o n policies and our distorted asylum-granting system,

> "To the dangers of continued mass immigration ... can be added another, affecting the developing countries themselves. A young acquaintance, who recently spent two years teaching in Tanzania, tells me that he did not meet one local under 40 whose sole ambition was not to secure a ticket to the West, a situation that probably prevails in other Third World countries. That being so, permission to settle here helps to strip these countries of their most gifted people. The present, in effect, indulgent immigration policies of Western governments represent nothing less than a middle-term formula for a worldwide catastrophe. The only sound way forward for the West is to help the peoples of the Third World to raise their living standards in their own countries."
>
> J. Pearson, *Daily Telegraph*, January 8, 1997.

those most dissatisfied with the situation in the home countries try to leave, instead of changing the situation at home. Cuba, for example, remains a communist country because many of those who want to overthrow its government are not there, but here in the United States. Just like brain drain, dissident drain reinforces the negative conditions that make people want to leave the sending countries.

> "There's nothing we could ever do — we could take 3 million, 5 million a year; we could completely destroy the environmental resources of this country; we could completely destroy the job markets; we could destroy the social fabric of this nation — there's no way that we could ever relieve the pressure [on people in the sending countries] by immigration. .... The only hope for most of the impoverished people in the world to be helped where they live, to bloom where they are planted."
>
> Roy Beck, *Immigration by the Numbers*, 1996.

A Drop in the Bucket. The number of immigrants we admit is enormous: over 900,000 people in 1996 alone — enough, certainly, to disrupt life in the United States. Yet, it is a vanishing fraction of the number of people whose lot would be improved by coming here; 4.6 billion people in the world live in countries where the average annual income is less than one tenth of that in the United States. Our humanitarian efforts would be better spent on improving conditions in the sending countries, rather than squandered on dramatically improving the lives of an infinitesimal fraction of their natives.

No Safety Valve. Nor does our immigration policy actually help the sending countries with their excess population problems. The million-a-year we take in is dwarfed by the number of people who want to come to the United States (400 million, according to the International Gallup poll). And the world population increases by around

90 million more people every year; to put it another way, 90

> "The prospect of being able to immigrate to the United States — legally or illegally — may actually increase suffering because it allows high fertility countries to put off taking action on overpopulation[.] If our impulses that seem in the short run to do good lead ultimately to worldwide disaster and most quickly to disaster in the countries we wish to help, they are not humanitarian. Not tightening our borders is destructive because it blocks environmental feedback that should be a warning sign of limits."
> Virginia Abernethy, *U.S. Immigration Fuels World-Wide Population Growth*, 1994.

times faster than we admit immigrants.   The fractional amount of excess population that is siphoned off from sending countries does nothing to help their growing populations.   Meanwhile, it sends our population growth soaring as well: immigration has been responsible for 50 percent of our population growth since 1970.   Thus our immigration policy worsens, not improves, the world population problem.

Social Ruination. In some cases, the immigration to the U.S. from some countries does serious damage to the social structures of the communities left behind. A 1993 study by Nelly Salgado de Snyder published in the Hispanic Journal of Behavioral Sciences describes towns desolated by emigration of their young men and pushed to the brink of extinction, which worsens the pressure to migrate. The small amounts of money the migrant men send home in remittances cannot compensate for the devastation caused by their wholesale absence.

> "Yes, they have raised their lives a bit economically, but it is a pity, the divided houses we have here. The people morally, psychologically, have many problems. The families lose control, they lose unity, they lose the sense of being families. Every year more people leave. Every year the towns are more and more alone."
> Fr. Samuel Fernandez Espinosa, "Exodus of Men Haunts Mexico,"
> *San Jose Mercury News,*
> August 15, 1993.

Other Population-Environmental Quotes

"Our physical habitat is being threatened by an immigration flow that represents only 1 percent of Third World annual population growth....Americans must trade a national vision of beckoning Statue of Liberty and a vision of wide-open spaces for a more realistic one of a world of limits and constraints."
B. Meredith Burke, "A Statue With Limitations", *Newsweek*, February 24, 1994.

"We can never have a sane immigration policy until we have a sane population policy. The ideal mix of births and immigrants is a difficult question that must be solved by public debate. Our view is that immigration adds important variety to our population and permits the United States to give refuge to people who really need it. So our preference would be to maintain a reasonable level of immigration and compensate for it with fewer births."
Paul and Anne Erlich, *Elephants in the Volkswagen*, 1990.

"The United States must develop a population policy leading toward shrinkage, and that means the number of births plus immigrants must be slightly below the number of deaths plus emigrants. Basically, for every immigrant admitted, a birth must be forgone. How the mix of births and immigrants is achieved is not a scientific issue, but one to be decided by democratic choice".
Paul and Anne Erlich, *Elephants in the Volkswagen*, 1990.

"Immigration is a very complex and ethically difficult issue. I agree that not all environmental groups should become involved with immigration. But I believe that every environmental group does have an obligation to make the obvious need to reduce U.S. population size, lower our levels of wasteful consumption, and develop more efficient, environmentally benign technologies part of its policy stance. And part of that stance should be to point out the necessary trade-off between births and immigrants".
Paul and Anne Erlich, *Elephants in the Volkswagen*, 1990.

"...[Population policy must be policy for a nation, not for the whole world, because there is no world sovereignty to back up a global policy. We can, and should, seek to persuade other nations to take steps to control their population growth; but our primary focus should be on the population growth within our own borders. This means that overpopulation can be avoided only if borders are secure; otherwise poor and overpopulated nation will export their excess to richer and less populated nations."
Garrett Hardin, *Living Within Limits*, 1993.

"...we must be forthright in identifying immigration reforms as part of our goal to stabilize global and national populations. An increasing population, regardless of the reason for the increase, uses more resources and produces more pollution. Those interested in the conservation of natural resources and the protection of ecological systems for all people must be free to discuss immigration issues from this perspective, without the fear of being labeled racist or bigoted."
Izaak Walton League 'Environments for Life', Winter 1994.

"It is time to understand 'the environment' for what it is: the national-security issue of the early twenty-first century. The political and strategic impact of surging populations, spreading disease, deforestation and the soil erosion, water depletion, air pollution, and, possibly, rising sea levels in critical, overcrowded regions like the Nile Delta and Bangladesh—developments that will prompt mass migration and, in turn, incite group conflicts—will be the core foreign policy challenge from which most others will ultimately emanate, arousing the public and uniting assorted interests left over from the Cold War."
Robert Kaplan in his article "The Coming Anarchy", *The Atlantic Monthly*, February 1994.

"As earth adds to its total population by nearly 95,000,000 people each year, the pressure upon environments and resources grows greater, the pace of illegal immigration quickens, and entire societies in the developing world collapse under the strain."
Paul Kennedy, Yale professor, in *Financial Times*.

"I really believe California is probably growing too fast, too big, and at some point there will be a time of reckoning."
Manuel Lujan, then Secretary of the Interior Department, whose water projects provide much of the state's water, *The Fresno Bee*, March 13, 1991.

"Immigration is the driving force behind the disastrous population growth that is destroying our environment, and the quality of our lives. Our country's population already far exceeds the long range carrying capacity of its resources and

environment, yet we continue to grow rapidly. Consequently, our top priority must be to halt, and eventually to reverse, the growth of our population so that it can fall to a smaller and more sustainable level, in balance with our resources and environment."
Donald Mann, NPG Press Release, October 19, 1994.

"In 1917 the total number of Americans passed 100 million, after three full centuries of steady growth. In 1967 — just half a century later — the 200 million mark was passed. If the present rate of growth continues, the third hundred million persons will be added in roughly a thirty-year period. This means that by the year 2000, or shortly thereafter, there will be more than 300 million Americans. The growth will produce serious challenges for our society. I believe that many of our present social problems may be related to the fact that we have had only fifty years in which to accommodate the second hundred million Americans...."
President Richard Nixon, *Special message to the U.S. Congress on problems of Population Growth,* July 18, 1969.

"[Dramatically reduced U.S. population densities would insure individual prosperity and quality environment for future generations."
David Pimentel, professor in the College of Agriculture and Life Sciences at Cornell University, and Marcia Pimentel, Senior Lecturer in the College of Human Ecology at Cornell University.

"...no substantial benefits will result from further growth of the nation's population; [it is] rather that the gradual stabilization of our population would contribute

significantly to the nation's ability to solve its problems."
[Population then was about 200 million.]
Rockefeller Commission, *Report of the Commission on Population Growth and the American Future*, March 27, 1972.

"The message of Europe's battle for the soul of environmentalism could not be more clear: if progressive and mainstream public interest groups do not address the taboo questions of tackling surging populations, the extreme right wing certainly will."
Mark Schapiro, *The Amicus Journal*, Winter 1992.

"The United States can take its place alongside China, Nigeria, Indonesia and India in claiming the global power and prestige that vast populations automatically confer. Wretched and infertile Japan and Germany will just have to content themselves with trade and technological ascendancy, skyrocketing productivity and superior standards of living."
David Simcox, *Washington Times*, May 25, 1990.

"Immigrant demand [for homes], if it keeps up, could underpin vibrant growth in the housing market for the rest of the decade. Largely because of immigration, the US population by the year 2000 is expected to number 25 million more than it was in 1990. That's the equivalent of having Canada move to the United States. We're looking at one of the largest decades of population growth in United States history."
Larry Small, Reuters, "Immigration Seen Giving Boost to U.S. Homebuying."

"The level of economic development for Blacks had gone up for 40 years under tight labor policy, low immigration. For the last 25 years—loose labor, high immigration—the situation for Blacks has been going down. ... The big question the American people have to ask their politicians is: what's your plan? If the politician is voting to keep the status quo, keep these numbers of immigrants coming, what is their plan for handling 130 million more people over the next half century? The fact is nobody has a plan."

Roy Beck, author of *Re-Charting America's Future*, on *BorderLine*, February 15, 1996.

How to See Through Your Opponents' Arguments

How to See Through Your
Opponents' Arguments

As important as it is to be able to construct your own immigration arguments, it is sometimes not enough. Sometimes, particularly when in debate, it is also important to be able to see through your opponents' arguments.

Since your opponent is wrong, most of his arguments are going to be based on wrong information or false reasoning. Wrong information can be countered with right information (much of which we have provided you in the previous sections). False reasoning is a little trickier to counteract, so let's examine some of the most common fallacies found in arguments.

Fallacies (that is, structural errors in reasoning) are not obscure rhetorical devices, leftovers from forensics classes of the past. No, fallacies are alive and well—and thriving in the immigration debate. Opponents of immigration reform use them constantly as their chief weapons for blocking critical discussion of our country's immigration policy. A familiarity with some common fallacies may help you to identify them in the arguments of others and avoid them in arguments of your own.

What follows is a brief introduction to major fallacies in general and to their use in the immigration debate in particular. [74]

---

[74]We had to rename some of the fallacies for you, because they are usually called by their Latin names. However, all of these fallacies are standard in informal logic, and have been for hundreds of years.

FALLACY NO. 1:
STARTING WITH THE ANSWER

There is no surer way to reach a particular conclusion than by beginning with it, which is easily remembered as Starting with the Answer (SWA). Starting with the Answer is what's called a causal fallacy, that is, it confuses the relationship of cause to effect.

A famous example of SWA comes from the pen of St. Anselm. One of the foremost thinkers of his day, Anselm was not content to rely on faith in God, but sought to prove God's existence. (His attempt is called the ontological argument for the existence of God, put forth in his book *Proslogium* in the 1080s). His reasoning went as follows:

> *God is, by definition, greater than anything.*
> *A God that exists is greater than one that doesn't.*
> *If God didn't exist, He wouldn't be greater than anything.*
> *Therefore, God must exist.*

Obviously, Anselm is cheating. He has built his answer into his initial assumption; in effect, he defines God in such a way as to necessitate His existence.[75]

The above might seem to be too obvious to you. Who could be fooled by such specious reasoning? Answer: lots of people. Besides, SWA is often more subtle. As a result,

---

[75]Don't worry; Anselm didn't get away with it. The contemporary monk Gaunilo of Marmoutier, in his book *Liber pro insipiente*, refuted the ontological argument. In reply, Anselm wrote a sequel to the *Proslogium*, in which he simply repeated his original argument.

80

controlling the argument by controlling the initial assumptions or definitions is more common than you might think. Does this argument sound familiar?

> *America is a nation of immigrants.*
> *If we stop taking in immigrants, we won't be*
> *a nation of immigrants any more.*
> *If we're not a nation of immigrants any more,*
> *we won't be America any more.*
> *To remain America, we must continue taking*
> *in immigrants.*

Just as St. Anselm's faith in God enticed him to fallacy, so too the faith that some people have in immigration blinds them to their errors in reasoning.

Fallacy No. 2:
The Irrelevant Conclusion

Another causal fallacy is the ever-popular Irrelevant Conclusion. In a sense, Irrelevant Conclusion is the opposite of Starting with the Answer. In SWA, you strive to build your answer into the premises of your argument; in Irrelevant Conclusion, you pull your conclusion out of thin air—that is, your conclusion has nothing to do with your premises at all.

Sound far fetched? Not really. When's the last time you watched a commercial for soft drinks, or for blue jeans? The "proof" that is presented in the commercial rarely has anything to do with the product itself. You hear some form of Irrelevant Conclusion every election-time:

> *I love my children;*
> *I have never missed a day's work;*

I served my country in wartime;
I believe in the divine nature of America's
destiny;
So vote for me in November.

The points are interesting; they may arguably say something about the character of the candidate (like, he's an ordinary parent with good health who got drafted). But the conclusion that he is the appropriate person to elect to office comes out of nowhere.

Even a casual listen to immigrationist argument will turn up Irrelevant Conclusion:

Immigrants are colorful and add to our
diversity;
Immigrants only come here to better their
lives and mean no one harm;
Immigrants evince family values;
Immigrants pay tribute to the greatness of
country by wanting to come here;
Therefore, the number of annual immigrants
should not be reduced.

The premises (if you accept them) might lead to some conclusion; perhaps that immigrants are well-meaning. But the conclusion that immigration reform is not necessary does not follow from them.

FALLACY NO. 3:
THE RIGID RULE

As a general rule, rules are good. But you can have too much of a good thing. Rules are not absolutes, and cannot be applied unthinkingly to every situation. The Rigid Rule is a fallacy caused by overadherence to a rule or principle.

Courts must avoid The Rigid Rule all the time when trying to apply rules (the laws) to specific situations (cases). For example, the prohibitions against murder cannot be rigidly applied; the courts waive them in cases of self-defense. A famous example of the courts avoiding The Rigid Rule comes from Justice Oliver Wendell Holmes:

> "The most stringent protection of free speech
> would not protect a man in falsely shouting
> fire in a theatre and causing a panic."
>
> *Schenck v. United States* (1919).

As a general rule, one has freedom of speech. But the court recognized that that rule must be modified in circumstances where speech is used to endanger the public.

Because rules make things simple, they are very attractive; thus, The Rigid Rule can be very seductive. Immigrationist use this allure to their advantage:

> *Hardworking people are good for the economy;*
> *Immigrants are hardworking people;*
> *So immigrants are good for the economy.*

Hardworking people are, in general, good for the economy. And let's assume all immigrants are hardworking people. But that doesn't mean that any quantity of hardworking immigrants is good for the economy. The economy is not so simple that one rule can cover it. Look at it another way:

> *Prunes are good for you* (they are, certainly
> compared with junk food*);*

*The more good things you eat, the better off
you are* (this is true);
*The more prunes you eat, the better off you
are* (this not true, as anyone who has ever
eaten a great many prunes will tell you).

Fallacy No. 4:
Hasty Generalization

Hasty Generalization is the opposite of The Rigid
Rule. In The Rigid Rule, you misapply a general rule to a
specific situation; in Hasty Generalization, you generalize a
specific situation into a sweeping rule. Like The Rigid Rule,
Hasty Generalization is an instance of oversimplifying an
issue.

If you went to Paris for a weekend, and decided you
didn't like it because it rains too much, you would be guilty
of Hasty Generalization. It was probably just rainy that
weekend. Two days is not enough information from which to
generalize a city's weather. If you went to Seattle for a week
and made the same conclusion, you would still be committing
Hasty Generalization. Just because you would happen to be
correct (Seattle is very rainy) doesn't alter the fact that the
generalization from two days to all year is a hasty one.

Similarly, three immigrants are not sufficient reason
to form a rule about all immigrants:

> *Albert Einstein, John Lennon, and Peter
> Brimelow have been good for our society.*
> *Albert Einstein, John Lennon, and Peter
> Brimelow are immigrants.*
> *Immigrants are good for our society.*

84

Sometimes the argument is less specific: "Some immigrants start Fortune 500 companies, are valedictorians, and have 32 percent fewer cavities than Americans." Perhaps, but to extrapolate from those few to the effect of the 24 million immigrants in the United States is clearly a Hasty Generalization.

FALLACY NO. 5:
CONFUSING COINCIDENCE AND CAUSALITY

Confusing Coincidence and Causality is a causal fallacy. Although the name is a mouthful, it is simple to understand: just because two things happen to coincide doesn't mean one causes the other. For example:

> *Whenever I carry an umbrella my allergies are better;*
> *To improve my allergies, I should always carry an umbrella.*

Now, it may in fact be true that whenever I carry an umbrella my allergies are better. But that does not mean that my allergies are better **because** I am carrying an umbrella.[76] This confusion of coincidence and causality forms the basis for many superstitions.

In immigration debate, it often sounds like this:

---

[76]That does not necessarily mean the two are unrelated. In this case, the two factors may have a common cause: I am carrying an umbrella because it's raining, and when it rains the pollen count goes down, improving my allergies.

*After our huge wave of immigration at the
turn of the century, America went on to
greatness.*
*Therefore, the greatness of our country
depends on immigration.*

The first statement may be true. But it does not stand
to reason that that greatness was caused by the immigration.
In fact, that greatness may have been achieved despite the
immigration; or perhaps the optimum conditions that formed
the foundation of greatness also attracted immigrants at the
same time. In any case, to jump to the conclusion that
immigration is a key to our country's greatness is
unwarranted. This fallacy is a favorite of immigrationist
Julian Simon, who argues that because materials indicators
(such as the cost of raw materials and standard of living) have
gotten better over the last fifty years while the population has
been skyrocketing, the only possible conclusion is that the
more people we have the better off we are.

The Appeals

When someone really doesn't have a leg to stand on,
or is too lazy to craft a causal fallacy, he often resorts to an
Appeal; that is, he appeals to emotion instead of reason. The
Appeals are very handy when there isn't a lot of time for
debate, and are often heard before large audiences. They are
an attempt to get you feeling instead of thinking, because if
you start thinking, you may start thinking for yourself.

Appeal No. 1:
The Appeal to Popularity

Since some people feel it is more important to be popular than either right or good, they often appeal to the popularity of an idea to get you to buy into it. "*E.T.* must be a great film; everybody's seeing it," is very similar to "Everyone likes the idea of immigration, so it must be a good thing." Now, there could be a lot of reasons that many people have seen *E.T.* (like, they had to take their children to see it); it is not necessarily a great film. So too, many people might like immigration because it makes them feels good about the desirability of our nation; but that doesn't make immigration necessarily a good thing for the country. Appeal to popularity is nothing more than peer pressure.

Appeal No. 2:
The Appeal to Force

The appeal to force boils down to "Agree with me or you'll be in trouble." When immigrationists argued that Washington D.C. should grant suffrage to aliens living there, one of the reasons was that without the right to vote, the aliens might take to the streets in frustration, as they did in the Mt. Pleasant Riots. Force may indeed be a motivator for going along with someone; but it doesn't make them right. Appeal to force may also be thought of as coercion, or an appeal to fear.

Appeal No. 3:
The Appeal to Deference

The appeal to deference relies on your willingness to defer to important people on all sorts of matters, whether they know better than you or not. Madison Avenue relies on this appeal heavily: Whoopi Goldberg plugs MCI, Candice Bergen plugs Sprint, and Bill Cosby plugs Jello. These actors are not experts either in telecommunications or gelatinous foodstuffs; yet their celebrity is expected to influence you in such matters. The same thing happens when immigrationists cite "a survey of economists" or quote Bill Gates as proof that immigration is good for the country. Economists may have some idea what expands (but not improves) the economy; and Bill Gates probably has an idea what's good for Bill Gates. But citing them as experts on the benefits of immigration to the country is just an appeal to deference.

APPEAL NO. 4:
THE APPEAL TO PITY

When your spouse comes home, and begins to argue that the venetian blinds should be closed slanting up instead of down (for no particular reason), and finally says "Just humor me, I've had a hard day," he is using the appeal to pity. If the appeal is blatant enough, it can be funny: we all know the joke about the teenager who killed his parents, and then begged for mercy from the court because he was an orphan.

Almost any newspaper article on immigration will make an appeal to pity (usually at the beginning): *widowed Maria Vargas, who works two jobs and sews her own clothes, only wants to make a better life for her baby girl. She heard that, in America, if she works hard, she can give her daughter the life she could only dream of as a child.* By focusing of our emotions on the plight of the individual, the author distracts from the overall effect of a million Maria Vargases. Journalism call this human interest; logicians call it an appeal to pity.

SUMMARY

Let's review. The Fallacies you should be on the look-out for are:

1. Starting with the Answer, and its opposite,
2. Irrelevant Conclusion;
3. Rigid Rule, and its opposite,
4. Hasty Generalization;
5. Coincidence & Causality;

and the Appeals:
6. Appeal to Popularity,
7. Appeal to Force,
8. Appeal to Deference,
9. Appeal to Pity.

One word to the wise. We have focused here on being able to see these fallacies in the arguments of the opponents of immigration reform. But just as we should be wary of fallacies in their arguments, we should beware of using fallacies in our own.

When you notice that your opponent is using a fallacy, you could simply point it out, and undermine his case that way. However, that does not work very well in many environments and for many audiences. Comments like, "I draw your attention to the fact that my opponent has committed the fallacy of confusing coincidence with causality," are probably not the best way to reach the man in street.

So, what can you do to counteract an opponent who seems to be "cheating" by using fallacy to his advantage?

You can read the following chapter.

How to Ruin Your
Opponents'
Arguments

HOW TO RUIN YOUR
OPPONENTS' ARGUMENTS

When you find yourself in the midst of the immigration debate, it would be a lot easier to survive (and win) if you had every fact, every figure, every study, every quote, and every argument memorized and at your mental fingertips. Unfortunately, this doesn't happen to anybody, even the most avid supporters of immigration reform.

But while an enormous stockload of statistical ammunition will help you against you opponents, it isn't always necessary. Below are some strategies you can rely on that require little memorization on your part. They are also effective because they allow you to use your opponent's own argument against him.

We will look at:

- ▸ exposing your opponent's argument by comparison;
- ▸ constructing a dilemma for your opponent; and
- ▸ reducing your opponent's argument to absurdity.

As a special bonus, we will look at examples of twenty of the most common arguments of reform opponents, and how you can reply to them.

ATTACK BY ANALOGY:
EXPOSING YOUR OPPONENT'S ARGUMENT
BY A COMPARISON

An easy way to show that your opponent's argument is silly is by comparing it to a similar, but more obvious, argument (often called an Analogy Attack). Here's an example:

> *Hardworking people are good for the economy;*
> *Immigrants are hardworking people;*
> *So immigrants are good for the economy.*

Opponent's Fallacy

> *Prunes are good for you;*
> *The more good things you eat, the better off you are;*
> *The more prunes you eat, the better off you are).*

Attack by Analogy

Sound familiar? It should, since it's from the previous chapter. The previous chapter is loaded with Analogy Attacks. In order to expose the fallacies as we listed them, we made similar arguments, using different terms, to show how wrong they were.

Analogy is a lively way of exposing the flaw in your opponent's argument (in the case above, the failure to recognize that it is possible to get too much of a good thing). Analogies also make it easier for your audience to grasp ideas that are hard to get a hold on otherwise.

SAMPLE ANALOGY NO. 1: NURSES AND PIZZA

Here's another example.

*Imagine you go home tonight and there's too little food in the pantry to make dinner. You could go grocery shopping, but you're hungry **now**. So you do the simplest thing: you order*

*a pizza. The pizza eaten, you are stuffed, and
so don't feel like grocery shopping. The next
night when you go home, there will still be too
little food in the pantry to make dinner.*

What's all that got to do with immigration, you ask?
The situation above is an analogy to American dependence on
foreign labor. In the 1980s, a nursing shortage was felt (*we
were hungry but the pantry was bare*); we could have allowed
the shortage to drive supply-and-demand, where the need for
nurses causes their wages to rise, increasing the desirability of
the profession, and drawing more students into nursing
careers, and solving the nursing shortage (*take the time and
inconvenience of going to the grocery store, so we can make
dinner for ourselves*). But instead we brought in foreign
workers (*hired somebody outside to make dinner for us*). The
end result: continued nursing shortage (*there's still too little
food in the pantry*).

Can't you get people to understand things like labor
dependence by discussing it directly? Well, yes, you can. But
getting them to understand it through analogy has several
advantages:

▸   it's fast;
▸   it's easier for most people to understand;
▸   it's much more memorable;
▸   it's hard to argue against it.

As the above example shows, analogies are useful not
only for countering an opponent, but, more generally, for
making your points. Let's take a look at another one, this
time with the immigration situation first.

Sample Analogy No. 2:
Mops and Bathtubs

You are discussing immigration with someone, who recognizes that it is causing some problems. However, her answer to the problem is that more effort and money must be directed at helping immigrants assimilate and pull their own weight, so that everyone benefits. Her husband chimes in, saying that he thinks we should just stop mollycoddling immigrants with bilingual education, foreign-language ballots, and welfare benefits. Although you feel the force of their remarks, you think they are focused on the wrong end of the problem. What can you say?

> *If you two went home tonight to find the tap in the bathtub was on, and the bathtub overfilling with water, what would you do first: clean up the mess, or turn off the tap?*

The answer is obvious to anyone: you turn off the tap first, and then deal with the mess. In others words, you handle the cause of the problem first, and then handle the effects. Through such an analogy, your friends might be able to see that if the flow of immigration is causing too many messy spillovers, then the tap needs to be dealt with first. Whether to use a mop or a bucket instead to clean up the mess is not as important as stopping the cause of the mess.

Just to show you that such analogies are actually used in the public debate over this issue:

> "Miss [Linda] Chavez espouses the precarious Beltway Conservative Establishment line: 'Immigration is fine; we just need to work on

assimilation.' Yeah. But doctors joke about a test for insanity: Put someone in a room with an overflowing sink and a mop. And then see if he tries to mop up the mess—or just turns off the tap. "

Peter Brimelow, "Unnatural Processes," *National Review*, April 7, 1997.

SAMPLE ANALOGY NO. 3:
SNOWFLAKES AND SNOWSTORMS

Someone accuses you of being "anti-immigrant" or xenophobic. You're frustrated because you're tired of any legitimate concerns over mass immigration being dismissed in this way. But you don't want to alienate this person any further. What can you say?

> *Hey, I like snow. Nothing is more invigorating than a gentle snow, and nothing more beautiful than an individual snowflake. But when snow starts to accumulate in drifts, when there's a snowstorm, it's a problem. You don't have to dislike snow to be concerned about a snowstorm.*

Credit goes to former Colorado governor Dick Lamm for this firm but gentle analogy.

SAMPLE ANALOGY NO. 4:
HAYSTACKS AND NEEDLES

Your analogies don't have to be as original or clever as Governor Lamm's. A good old-fashioned cliche will often work just as well.

Your business-booster buddy squawks that if immigration is cut back, business will lose access to 'the best and the brightest', and edge we desperately need to stay competitive in the global economy. You know that barely 6 percent of immigrants are skill-based admissions, and that most immigrants are poor and low-skilled. What do you say?

> *Only a few thousand of the 900,000 immigrants we admit every year are high-skilled types. Are you telling me we have to buy a haystack in order to get a needle?*

Original? No. Elaborate? No. Effective? Yes. An analogy like "a needle in a haystack" is already so familiar to your audience that no further elaboration is needed.

A WORD OF CAUTION

A word of caution about analogies is in order: workers ain't prunes, nurses ain't pizza, and low-skilled immigrants ain't hay. Don't get so carried away in an analogy that you forget this. No analogy is perfect; they all "break down" if pushed too far. Keep in mind that the only purpose in using the analogy is to make the underlying point, and you won't get trapped by the limits of your analogy.

A ROCK AND A HARD PLACE: CONSTRUCTING A DILEMMA FOR YOUR OPPONENT

One of the best ways to undo your opponents (or simply to make your own point) is with a tactic called **the dilemma**. In essence, you frame the discussion so that your opponents is "darned if he does" and "darned if he doesn't."

In a dilemma, you set up two alternatives and then show that either leads to the same conclusion — the one you want to reach. That's a little dry, so let's look at an example, say, in the economic area of the debate.

> Generally, a dilemma sounds like this:
> *Either A or B;*
> *If A, then C;*
> *if B, then C;*
> *Therefore, C.*

Let's suppose you are trying to make the point the immigration is not what we need for our economy. Without wheeling out cartloads of statistics and studies, you could say:

Either immigrants have the job skills our economy needs, or they don't.

If they do, then we are using immigrants to do work we are at present unable to do ourselves. In that way, we are becoming dependent on foreign labor. By bringing in immigrants to supply labor, we are not allowing our own system of supply and demand the time to adjust, and to develop own our people or methods of doing what needs done. Thus, because immigration makes us less likely to develop our own people and resources, immigration is not good for our economy.

If they don't, then they are duplicating our own labor resources, competing with our own

98

people. By increasing the supply of labor, they lower its value; that is, wages are depressed. Low-skilled workers' wages go down, while high-skilled workers are less affected; thus, the poor get poorer and the gap between the rich and the poor grows, shrinking the middle class. Because immigration creates labor surplus and further shrinks the middle class, immigration is not good for our economy.

In either case, immigration is not good for our economy.

The case is a bit simplified, but illustrative. Note that no matter which alternative you pick, you wind up with the same conclusion: that immigration is not good for the economy.

Here's another example, this one from the tradition area of the immigration debate.

Either our present level of immigration is in line with our tradition or it isn't.

If it is, then we must realize how severely our society has changed from the empty continent we had 200 years ago. No longer do we have the traditional need for people for territorial expansion and new settlements. Thus, to keep immigration policy current with the times, we must reduce the level of immigration.

If it isn't, then we have allowed immigration policy to deviate from the successful policies of the past, and we must return to a traditional level of immigration, like the lower levels we had in the past.

In either case, we must lower the level of immigration.

Now go back and take a look at the first two arguments used in this manual, *Tradition Argument No.1* and *Tradition Argument No. 2*. Read carefully and you will notice that, taken together, they are a dilemma. In fact, they are the very same dilemma as the example above—just a little more elaborate.

It is not always easy to construct a dilemma; it takes some forethought and some mental elbow grease. The effort does pay off, however, since dilemmas are very powerful arguments with a strong air of commonsense to them. They give structure to your case, make it easier to remember your next point, and tend to make you sound more sensible than your opponent.

MAKING YOUR OPPONENT LOOK FOOLISH: TRAVELING TO THE ABSURD

Remember your greatest advantage in the immigration debate: you are right, and your opponent is wrong. Now, it's hard to prove you're right; it is always hard to prove anything positive. But it is easy to prove that someone else is wrong. So one of the best ways to undo your opponent is by following his arguments through to their natural conclusion.

Since your opponent is wrong, this should lead to some absurdity or contradiction.

Let's take a look at how this might work. Your opponent says "immigration should not be lowered because immigrants are hard-working, moral people who are good for our economy and society." Your first instinct, of course, is to contradict him and chide him for such oversimplification. But, what happens if, instead, you travel along with him for a minute in his line of reasoning?

Okay, you say, let's assume for a minute that he is right, and the million immigrants a year we are admitting are good for our economy and society. Well, if one million immigrants are good, why stop there? Wouldn't two million immigrants be twice as good? You can't have too much of a good thing? While we're at it, why shouldn't we admit five, ten, twenty, forty millions immigrants a year, as long as they are so good for our country? Is that what your opponent is advocating? Or is there a point at which we can have too much of a good thing?

At this stage, your opponent is in trouble. If he agrees that the number of people we should admit is limitless, he seems absurd to your audience. If he doesn't, he is admitting that, regardless how wonderful immigrants may be, it is possible to have too many of them—which is just the point you are trying to make. Even if he says that the number we are getting now is "just right," you can then ask him whether he supports a cap on immigration at the current level (especially since immigration has been rising in the last year or two).

By following through on your opponent's position to any absurd implications, you make his position look foolish and make your own point in the bargain.

Common Arguments You Are Likely To Encounter

Whatever your level of involvement or interest in immigration reform, you've probably heard the arguments against it repeatedly. Well, here they are again.

Below are some of the most common arguments you are likely to come up against in the immigration debate, following by brief refutations. Other books have done this sort of thing for you[77]; in fact, the sample arguments earlier in this book refute many of the assertions below. For that reasons, the replies to the assertions will not be elaborate. They should, however, give you sense of the general tack your replies should take.

1.   *Immigration is a big part of American tradition and national character; we are uniquely a "nation of immigrants."*

> America was not founded by immigrants; it was founded by settlers, when we had a vast unoccupied continent, not a mature country like we have now. Furthermore, while immigration has been part of our past, it has not been so high.

2.   *Immigration has been good for us in the past and has made our nation great.*

> To the degree immigration has been beneficial in the past, it has been so because it was quite

---

[77]The author heartily recommends Roy Beck's *Re-Charting America's Future* and *The Case Against Immigration*, and Peter Brimelow's *Alien Nation*. All these books are available from the Social Contract Press, 316½ E. Mitchell Street Suite 4, Petoskey, Michigan, 49770; telephone 616–347–1171, fax 616–347–1185.

102

limited. History shows us that immigration at high levels is not beneficial, which is why the country stopped the Great Wave.

3.   *Throughout our history, people have always attacked immigrants and they have always been wrong.*

While people have opposed immigration for a variety of motives over the years, Americans have always had legitimate concerns about immigration, concerns about its effect on the population, the economy, the society. While some of their fears may have not come true in the past, that is largely because mass immigration to this country was stopped, not because their fears were unfounded.

4.   *We have had many years of high immigration in the past so today's levels aren't unusual.*

Before just recently, only six years of our two hundred year history saw as much immigration as we had in 1996 (not counting the amnesty admission of illegal immigrants in the late 1980s).

5.   *Actually, immigration is less of an influence or problem today because immigrants make up a lower percentage of the population than at times in the past.*

Quite the opposite is true. When there were fewer people in the country there was much more room and opportunity for immigrants. Now, in a country already stuffed with 242 million natives, having an additional 24 million immigrants is no small problem. The more people we have in the country, the fewer immigrants we can afford to have, not more.

6.   *Immigrants have good/better "family values" and make good/better citizens.*

> America was founded not on the very modern catchphrase of "family values", but rather on the ideals of rugged individualism. If you think there is something wrong with American values, you should work on "improving" Americans, not simply replace them with immigrants who you think are better than they are.

7.   *Immigrants revitalize neighborhoods and businesses.*

> To put it another way, heavy immigration maintains a steady inflow of poor people who can keep ghettoes going, instead of those areas becoming abandoned and ripe for redevelopment to improve the civic quality of life.

8.   *Greater cultural and ethnic diversity is better for us and strengthens our society.*

> World history—including today's newspapers —makes it clear that cultural and ethnic diversity can be a source of division and strife. While some diversity can be stimulating, it can be added only at the expense of our societal unity, which is already uncomfortably strained. For most Americans, more ethnic tension and economic dislocation are too high a price to pay so that the wealthy can enjoy exotic restaurants and cheap domestic help.

9.   *The U.S. has plenty of land and resources so we can easily handle today's level of immigration.*

> Land is not all that is required to sustain people. If it were, we could all live in the

Grand Canyon or the Arizona desert. At its present population, America has water and pollution problems enough to worry about without doubling its population growth through immigration.

10.   *Immigrants don't really have much impact in your state or in most parts of the country.*

Just because it isn't happening in your backyard doesn't mean you aren't affected. Immigrants cost a net $65 billion to the economy every year—who do you think is paying for that? Besides, in our mobile society, immigration in the U.S. is not an isolated phenomenon. More and more places are affected every day and, at the present speed of immigration, no one's community will remain untouched for long.

11.   *We have a moral and humanitarian duty to admit large numbers of immigrants.*

Our greatest moral obligation is to our fellow citizens; as long as there are still poor, undereducated, ill-fed, or unhoused Americans, we are not justified in adding to their numbers with citizens of other nations. And if we have a moral duty toward the citizens of other countries, we should focus on helping them make their countries more livable places for them to remain, not simply allow a small handful of their people to abandon their homelands, and then pat ourselves on the back for our "humanitarian" efforts.

12.   *People who are against more immigration are racist, nativist, etc.*

> Perhaps some are. There are always people who support the right idea for the wrong reason—but that does not make the idea wrong. And none of that changes the fact that bringing a million additional people from other countries to this one every year is tough on our economy, strains the fabric of society, and ruins any hope of reducing environmental damage by stabilizing our population.

13.   *Immigrants are an essential driving force behind our economy, performing jobs Americans won't do (e.g., farm labor), working harder than many Americans, having a better work ethic and attitude, being very entrepreneurial.*

> There are no jobs Americans won't do, only conditions and wages that are unacceptable. The employers and other businessfolk economically dependent on high levels of immigration and cheap labor are using this argument to justify a modern form of indentured servitude, and trying to shame Americans into accepting it.

14.   *Immigrants don't take jobs from Americans, they create more jobs.*

> Naturally, both are true. But many of those jobs are jobs in providing services to immigrants (such as social workers). What other jobs immigration does create are generally low-skilled (creating a drag on the development of the economy) and mostly go

to other immigrants anyway, not to Americans.

15.   *We live in a global economy and must have more foreign workers to be able to compete effectively in terms of numbers, skills, understanding of foreign markets, etc.*

Most of the people immigration imports into our labor market are just someone's poor relative from abroad, and do not exactly help us compete effectively or improve foreign markets. Very little immigration is of skilled personnel. Beside, it is precisely because of the global economy, and advances in worldwide technology, communication, and transportation that we do not have to allow people to move to the United States in order to take advantage of the talents and benefit from their contributions.

16.   *Immigrants are a big net benefit, paying taxes and contributing far more to our society than they cost.*

That kind of calculation works only if you start cutting out the immigrants' children; and refugees; and asylees; and immigrants who are not yet of working age; and immigrants who are past working age; and immigrants from certain countries (like Mexico); and immigrants who have been here for less than five or ten years. No one has yet explained how importing almost a million predominantly poor people into our economy every year can be a "big net benefit."

17.   *If we don't grow our workforce and population with immigrants, social security will go bankrupt.*

There are certainly problems with social
security caused by the population bulge of the
Baby Boom. But obviously the answer is not
to continue to grow the population, particularly with people who, when they are older,
will simply worsen the drain on social
security.

18.   *Immigrants catch up quickly economically and soon
blend in to American society.*

In today's atmosphere of multiculturalism,
there is much less encouragement for immigrants to assimilate. Today's schools do not
focus on assimilation as they used to.
Besides, the point is not that immigrants are
not assimilating as fast as they used to; the
point is that we are admitting immigrants at a
rate faster than they assimilate. As a result,
the body of unassimilated people in our
society grows, as does the social tension.

19.   *Restrictionists greatly overstate the degree to which
"chain migration" is a problem; actually, "family
reunification" is fair, morally right and consistent with
ensuring strong families and protecting "family values."*

Anyone who doesn't think chain migration is
a problem doesn't know that admissions in the
immediate relatives category are now seven
times higher than they were before it began.
Even if nepotism were an appropriate basis for
admissions in theory, in practice it would still
leave a lot to be desired. In essence, it is
immigrants who decide who will immigrate,
not natives. And, again, the answer to any

supposed problems with Americans is not to simply replace them with immigrants.

20.   *Illegal immigration is the only real problem—it's the illegals that are causing all the problems and they are who the public is concerned about.*

If the public is concerned mostly about illegal immigrants it is because they think most immigrants are illegal —they cannot believe the government would intentionally be admitting so many people.   Anyone who thinks that illegal immigration is the only real problem ignores two things: the effects of legal immigration aren't much different from the effects of illegal immigration; and there is three times as much legal immigration as illegal immigration.

TIPS ON
PRESENTING
YOURSELF AND
YOUR ARGUMENTS

Tips on Presenting Yourself and Your Arguments

So far in this book, we have focused on what to say to make your case for immigration reform. Now a few words on how to say it. You may have a cogent message, but if your delivery alienates your audience, it won't get through.

Volumes have been written on persuasive speaking, on "how to win arguments and influence people;" we cannot outdo them here. Still, a few of the following ideas may be useful to keep in mind, whether you are debating the issue of immigration reform on national television or at a cocktail party.

Talk to the Audience, Not to Your Opponent.

Do not try to convince your opponent he is wrong; this is usually a waste of time and effort. This is not an argument in a college coffee house. You are trying to reach your audience—citizens whose minds are not completely closed to the idea of immigration reform. Talk to them.

While a debating donnybrook with a hard-core opponent may be emotionally satisfying, it is generally not as productive as a reasonable but impassioned appeal to your audience's common sense.

Stay on the Topic.

This sounds easier to do than it is. Immigration stems into many interesting subjects: welfare, economics, language, politics, crime, etc. But in order to accomplish your goal of convincing people of the need for immigration reform you must focus on that alone. If you have a moderator, he may wander; you may want to wander into other interesting areas; your opponent is *planning* on wandering off the topic.

Try to resist this temptation. Even in the most informal setting, the clock is always ticking. You don't want to find at the end of your discussion about immigration reform that you have talked about almost everything but immigration reform.

TARGET YOUR AUDIENCE, IF POSSIBLE.

Not every audience will respond equally to the same arguments. An audience of fiscal conservatives may respond well to arguments about immigration's costs; an audience of social liberals might be more receptive to hearing about the threat immigration poses to opportunities for America's minorities and its poor. Find a viewpoint your audience can identify with, and proceed from there. Remember, where you start making your case is less important than that you come to the right conclusion.

Why you support immigration reform *may* be interesting to your audience; why *they* should support immigration reform will interest them even more.

REMAIN CALM.

If you get flustered or blow your top, you've lost. When people listen to you debate, they are more likely to remember how you acted than what you said. Remaining calm, while still retaining passion for the issue, shows that you are in control and inspires the trust of your audience.

How to S~~urvive~~ *Win* the
Immigration Debate

Remember Who Is Right.

You are—and right makes might. One of the best ways to stay focused is to remember that, and to rely on the strength of your conviction that immigration reform is necessary. Knowing that you are in the right will give you confidence; your audience can sense that, and it will help them have confidence in you too.

Immigrant Policy Is Not Immigration Policy.

Immigrant policy addresses the question: What shall we do about immigrants now that they are here? Immigration policy addresses the questions: How many people should be allowed to immigrate, who should they be, and what for? Debates about immigrant policy are a red herring; your opponents would love for you to focus on such issues. As long as everyone is focused on debating immigrant policy no one can do anything about immigration policy. Resist the urge to become sidetracked by the lively issues of immigrant policy[78], and always steer the debate back to immigration policy.

Give Your Opponent Some Rein.

As we have seen in previous sections, one of your best chances to succeed in the immigration debate is that your opponent will say something wrong or outrageous. If you

---

[78]These include such topics as bilingual education, bilingual ballots, and welfare for immigrants. These issues are important, no doubt about it. But don't allow your opponent to derail you into talking about these issues in order to keep you from talking about lowering the number of immigrants admitted each year.

constantly interrupt to prevent him from talking, you miss this opportunity—and may end up alienating your audience as well. Remember, you cannot refute your opponent's point until he makes it.

Don't get "stepped on."

On the other hand, don't give your opponent so much rein that he hangs you with it. Be certain that you speak up and make your points for immigration reform; otherwise, your opponent may talk endlessly, simply to prevent you from furthering your argument.

RECAP

This section will recap what we have gone over in this book: the immigration system (which is covered in the Appendix), making your immigration reform argument, recognizing the weaknesses in your opponent's arguments and how to use them, general debating tips.

IMMIGRATION SYSTEM OVERVIEW

OVERALL

The annual flow of immigration consists of two parts: legal and illegal. There is no theoretical limit to the number of legal immigrants admitted annually, because **the category of immediate relatives is unlimited.**

RELATIVES

The immediate relatives category includes unmarried minor children, spouses, and parents of U.S. citizens. Immediate relatives account for almost a quarter of all immigration, and for almost a third of all legal immigration. The immediate relatives category is unlimited; any individual who is the immediate relative of a U.S. citizen has a right to a visa under current immigration law, regardless of how many apply.

Other relatives fall into four subcategories called preferences. Sixty percent of the admissions for other relatives are taken up by the second preference (the spouses and unmarried children of lawful permanent residents).

	Categories	Quotas	1996
Relatives	*Immediate Relatives of U.S. Citizens*	*Unlimited*	302,000
	1st Pref.: Unmarried Adult Children of U.S. Citizens	*23,400*	21,000
	2nd Pref.: Spouses and Unmarried Adult Children of Legal Immigrants	*114,200*	183,000
	3rd Pref.: Married Adult Children of U.S. Citizens	*23,400*	25,000
	4th Pref.: Siblings of U.S. Citizens	*65,000*	65,000
Employment Based	*1st Pref.: Priority Workers*	*40,040*	28,000
	2nd Pref.: Professionally Exceptional	*40,040*	18,000
	3rd Pref.: Skilled Workers and Professionals	*40,040*	63,000
	4th Pref.: Special Immigrants	*9,940*	8,000
	5th Pref.: Investors	*9,940*	900
Lottery		*55,000*	58,000

EMPLOYMENT-BASED IMMIGRANTS

Employment-based immigrants are admitted because they are requested by employers. Half of all employed-based visas go not to workers, but to their dependent relatives.

REFUGEES AND ASYLEES

Refugees and asylees are applicants for admission who claim to be fleeing their homeland due to persecution on the basis of their political beliefs. Refugees apply from abroad and are subject to a numerical limit. Asylees apply from the within the U.S. and there is no limit to how many may apply or be granted asylum. Many more people apply for asylum than receive it. For example, in 1995, there were about 145,000 applications for asylum, but only 8000 were found to be legitimate. Many of these claims are from illegal aliens who simply seek to avoid deportation.

OTHER LEGAL IMMIGRANTS

Other legal immigrant categories include: the diversity visa lottery (with nearly 50,000), the special Cuban migration lottery (about 10,000), and some other groups (such as certain persons from the former Soviet Union). These special programs operate outside the core immigration programs mentioned above.

ILLEGAL ALIENS

Illegal aliens fall into two broad categories: those who come here temporarily, and those who come here to settle. The migrant illegals may number as many as three million a year; more precise figures are elusive. The settlers number at least 300,000 a year, by most estimates. The estimated number of illegal aliens living in the U.S. is 5,000,000.

Making Your Own Immigration Argument

The four main points in your central argument for immigration reform are:

Traditional. Our present immigration policy is not consistent with our immigration tradition
Economic. Immigration is not good for the economy.
Social. Too much immigration causes unhealthy social strain.
Population/Environmental. Immigration is an environmental/population problem.

Your argument should go roughly as follows: present immigration policy violates our immigration tradition; is damaging to the economy; causes social strain; and drives population growth and environmental degradation.

Seeing Through Your Opponents' Arguments

The fallacies you should be on the lookout for are:
- **Starting with the Answer**, and its opposite,
- **Irrelevant Conclusion**;
- **Rigid Rule**, and its opposite,
- **Hasty Generalization**;
- **Coincidence & Causality**;
- **Appeal to Popularity**,
- **Appeal to Force**,
- **Appeal to Deference**,
- **Appeal to Pity**.

118

HOW TO RUIN YOUR OPPONENTS'
ARGUMENTS

▸   construct a dilemma for your opponent;
▸   reduce your opponent's argument to absurdity;
▸   know the twenty of the most common arguments of reform opponents, and how you can reply to them (as follows):

1.   *Immigration is a big part of American tradition and national character; we are uniquely a "nation of immigrants".*

America was not founded by immigrants; it was founded by settlers, when we had a vast unoccupied continent, not a mature country like we have now. Furthermore, while immigration has been part of our past, it has not been so high.

2.   *Immigration has been good for us in the past and has made our nation great.*

To the degree immigration has been beneficial in the past, it has been so because it was quite limited. History shows us that immigration at high levels is not beneficial, which is why the country stopped the Great Wave.

3.   *Throughout our history, people have always attacked immigrants and they have always been wrong.*

While people have opposed immigration for a variety of motives over the years, Americans have always had legitimate concerns about immigration, concerns about its effect on the population, the economy, the society. While some of their fears may have not come true in the past, that is largely because mass immigration to this country was stopped, not because their fears were unfounded.

4.   *We have had many years of high immigration in the past so today's levels aren't unusual.*

Before just recently, only six years of our two hundred year history saw as much immigration as we had in 1996 (not counting the amnesty admissions of the late 1980s).

119

5.   *Actually, immigration is less of an influence or problem today because immigrants make up a lower percentage of the population than at times in the past.*

Quite the opposite is true. When there were fewer people in the country there was much more room and opportunity for immigrants. Now, in a country already stuffed with 242 million natives, having an additional 24 million immigrants is no small problem. The more people we have in the country, the fewer immigrants we can afford to have, not more.

6.   *Immigrants have good/better "family   values" and make good/better citizens.*

America was founded not on the very modern catchphrase of "family values," but rather on the ideals of rugged individualism. If you think there is something wrong with American values, you should work on "improving" Americans, not simply replace them with immigrants who you think are better than they are.

7.   *Immigrants revitalize neighborhoods and businesses.*

To put it another way, heavy immigration maintains a steady inflow of poor people who can keep ghettoes going, instead of those areas becoming abandoned and ripe for redevelopment to improve the civic quality of life.

8.   *Greater cultural and ethnic diversity is better for us and strengthens our society.*

World history—including today's newspapers —makes it clear that cultural and ethnic diversity can be a source of division and strife. While some diversity can be stimulating, it can be added only at the expense of our societal unity, which is already uncomfortably strained. For most Americans, more ethnic tension and economic dislocation are too high a price to pay so that the wealthy can enjoy exotic restaurants and cheap domestic help.

9.   *The U.S. has plenty of land and resources so we can easily handle today's level of immigration.*

Land is not all that is required to sustain people. If it were, we could all live in the Grand Canyon or the Arizona desert. At its present population, America has water and pollution problems enough to worry about without doubling its population growth through immigration.

10.   *Immigrants don't really have much impact in your state or in most parts of the country.*

Just because it isn't happening in your backyard doesn't mean you aren't affected. Immigrants cost a net $65 billion to the economy every year—who do you think is paying for that? Besides, in our mobile society, immigration in the U.S. is not an isolated phenomenon. More and more places are affected every day and, at the present speed of immigration, no one's community will remain untouched for long.

11. *We have a moral and humanitarian duty to admit large numbers of immigrants.*

Our greatest moral obligation is to our fellow citizens; as long as there are still poor, undereducated, ill-fed, or unhoused Americans, we are not justified in adding to their numbers with citizens of other nations. And if we have a moral duty toward the citizens of other countries, we should focus on helping them make their countries more livable places for them to remain, not simply allow a small handful of their people to abandon their homelands, and then pat ourselves on the back for our "humanitarian" efforts.

12. *People who are against more immigration are racist, nativist, etc.*

Perhaps some are. There are always people who support the right idea for the wrong reason—but that does not make the idea wrong. And none of that changes the fact that bringing a million additional people from other countries to this one every year is tough on our economy, strains the fabric of society, and ruins any hope of reducing environmental damage by stabilizing our population.

13. *Immigrants are an essential driving force behind our economy, performing jobs Americans won't do (e.g., farm labor), working harder than many Americans, having a better work ethic and attitude, being very entrepreneurial.*

There are no jobs Americans won't do, only conditions and wages that are unacceptable. The employers and other businessfolk economically dependent on high levels of immigration and cheap labor are using this argument to justify a modern form of indentured servitude, and trying to shame Americans into accepting it.

14. *Immigrants don't take jobs from Americans, they create more jobs.*

Naturally, both are true. But what jobs immigration does create are generally low-skilled (creating a drag on the development of the economy) and mostly go to other immigrants anyway, not to Americans.

15. *We live in a global economy and must have more foreign workers to be able to compete effectively in terms of numbers, skills, understanding of foreign markets, etc.*

Most of the people immigration imports into our labor market are just someone's poor relative from abroad, and do not exactly help us compete effectively or improve foreign markets. Very little immigration is of skilled personnel. Beside, it is precisely because of the global economy, and advances in worldwide technology, communication, and transportation that we do not have to allow people to move to the United States in order to take advantage of the talents and benefit from their contributions.

16.   *Immigrants are a big net benefit, paying taxes and contributing far more to our society than they cost.*

That kind of calculation works only if you start cutting out the immigrants' children; and refugees; and asylees; and immigrants who are not yet of working age; and immigrants who are past working age; and immigrants from certain countries (like Mexico); and immigrants who have been here for less than five or ten years. No one has yet explained how importing almost a million predominantly poor people into our economy every year can be a "big net benefit."

17.   *If we don't grow our workforce and population with immigrants, social security will go bankrupt.*

There are certainly problems with social security caused by the population bulge of the Baby Boom. But obviously the answer is not to continue to grow the population, particularly with people who, when they are older, will simply worsen the drain on social security.

18.   *Immigrants catch up quickly economically and soon blend in to American society.*

In today's atmosphere of multiculturalism, there is much less encouragement for immigrants to assimilate. Besides, the point is not that immigrants are not assimilating as fast as they used to; the point is that we are admitting immigrants at a rate faster than they assimilate. As a result, the body of unassimilated people in our society grows, as does the social tension.

19.   *Restrictionists greatly overstate the degree to which "chain migration" is a problem; actually, "family reunification" is fair, morally right and consistent with ensuring strong families and protecting "family values."*

Anyone who doesn't think chain migration is a problem doesn't know that admissions in the immediate relatives category are now seven times higher than they were before it began. Even if nepotism were an appropriate basis for admissions in theory, in practice it would still leave a lot to be desired. In essence, it is immigrants who decide who will immigrate, not natives. And, again, the answer to any supposed problems with Americans is not to simply replace them with immigrants.

20.   *Illegal immigration is the only real problem—it's the illegals that are causing all the problems and they are who the public is concerned about.*

If the public is concerned mostly about illegal immigrants it is because they think most immigrants are illegal —they cannot believe the government would intentionally be admitting so many people. Anyone who thinks that illegal immigration is the only real problem ignores two things: the effects of legal immigration aren't much different than the effects of illegal immigration; and there is three times as much legal immigration as illegal immigration.

Tips on Presenting Yourself
and Your Arguments

- ▸ **Talk to the audience, not to your opponent.**
- ▸ **Stay on the topic**.
- ▸ **Target your audience, if possible.**
- ▸ **Remain calm.**
- ▸ **Appearance matters.**
- ▸ **Remember who is right.**
- ▸ **Immigrant Policy is not Immigration Policy.**
- ▸ **Avoid ethnicities.**
- ▸ **Give your opponent some rein.**

Understanding the Immigration System

The immigration system can be confusing, even to those of us who work on it all the time. What follows is a brief overview of the immigration system that may help you keep it all straight.

The Federal Government and Immigration

Individual states cannot make laws to determine how many or what kind of people may immigrate to their domains. The federal government has exclusive authority over all immigration. That power derives from the Constitution, as a power of the nation. The idea that the national government is responsible for such things is inherent in the modern concept of nationhood. Court decisions have consistently reaffirmed this responsibility, which the federal government cannot delegate to states.

Congress, as the federal government's legislative branch, is responsible for making law to regulate immigration, which the executive branch must carry out. The executive branch's immigration duties are handled principally by an agency of the Justice Department called the Immigration and Naturalization Service (INS). The INS is responsible for processing requests for legal immigration, controlling illegal immigration, and administering immigration laws. It was created in 1891.

Other law enforcement agencies, such as local police, cannot enforce immigration laws. However, they can and are expected to cooperate with the INS's enforcement efforts if they become aware of a violation of immigration law.

How to ~~Survive~~ *Win* the Immigration Debate

Immigration Status

The people in the United States can be divided into two classes:

- the native-born (those who were citizens of the United States at birth)
- the foreign-born (those who were citizens of a foreign country at birth)

It is important not to confuse the term foreign-born with the term aliens, which denotes a more limited group. The term foreign-born includes even those aliens who have become citizens; the term alien does not include naturalized citizens.

Native-born

Natives are people who are citizens of the United States at birth. The following groups compose the native population:

- the children of U.S. citizens;
- the children of lawful permanent residents;
- the children of illegal aliens;
- some children of "multiple-status" couples.

The children of U.S. citizens are automatically citizens of the United States. This is the case regardless of whether the parents are native citizens or naturalized citizens. It also holds true when American citizens have a baby abroad.

The children of legal immigrants are also U.S. citizens. Lawful permanent residents are citizens of a foreign country who are allowed to live in the United States on a permanent basis. If they have children here, those children are automatically U.S. citizens.

The children of illegal aliens, if they are born within the boundaries of the United States, are given automatic citizen-ship at birth.

Children of citizens born abroad can also be U.S. citizens, under certain circumstances.

The Foreign-Born

Foreign-born designates all those who at birth were not citizens of the United States. Not everyone who is born in a foreign country is foreign-born. For example, if an American citizen couple goes abroad on vacation, and the wife gives birth in France, the baby is still a native-born American citizen. Similarly, not everyone who is born in the United States is a citizen. The U.S.-born children of foreign diplomats are not U.S. citizens, but rather are foreign-born.

The foreign-born consist of two groups:
· naturalized citizens;
· aliens.

Naturalized citizens are former aliens (or nationals) who have gone through the legal process of putting aside their previous citizenship, taking a new oath of allegiance and receiving American citizenship (a process called "naturalization").

Aliens refers broadly to people in the U.S. who are citizens of foreign countries and not of the United States.

The Three Types of Aliens

The term aliens refers broadly to people in the United States who are citizens of foreign countries and not of the United States. Aliens can be classified into three groups:
· nonimmigrants (such as visitors for pleasure; business visitors; temporary workers; foreign students; diplomats)
· legal immigrants;
· illegal aliens.

We will focus on these last two groups, legal immigrants and illegal aliens.

Legal Immigrants

Legal immigrants are aliens allowed to remain in the United States indefinitely. That is why they are also called "lawful permanent residents".

Legal immigrants fall into four broad categories:

- family-based immigrants (who have a relative who is a citizen or a lawful permanent resident)
- employment-based immigrants (who have an American employer to sponsor them and their dependents)
- lottery immigrants (who win a visa lottery for applicants who couldn't get in under the above categories)
- refugees and asylees (who claim to face individual persecution from their home government).

There is no limit to the number of legal immigrants who can be admitted every year. This is because one of the groups above (family-based immigrants) has no numerical ceiling. Categories of immigrants that have a numerical ceiling are said to be "capped". As long as any immigrant category remains uncapped, there can be no overall limit to the number of immigrants admitted annually.

The Family Preference System

In our present immigration system, priority is given to applicants for admission who have relatives in the United States. This policy is called family-based immigration, and unification of the entire extended family is the professed goal of the system. There are two things important to recognize about the family-based policy: first, it is essentially nepotistic; second, it sets an unattainable goal for immigration.

Family-based preference is nepotism; it admits people solely on the basis of who their relatives are, not on the basis of what they can contribute to U.S. society. In this respect, the policy is geared toward the benefit of the individual immigrants, not toward the benefit of the country as a whole. As a natural result, immigration is not as beneficial to the nation as it might be under a merit-based system.

Relative preference burdens our immigration system with an unreachable goal. Each immigrant who is admitted to reunite with his family here leaves more family members behind; they in turn apply for admission, and then their relatives become eligible. Thus, the number of people eligible for family preferences expands indefinitely. In consequence, the number of family-based immigrants keeps going up and the queue for admission continues to grow.

Family-based Preferences

It is important to note that the family-sponsored immigrants do not include immediate relatives. The immediate relative category is kept separate because it is not capped, whereas the family-sponsored categories are capped.

The four family-sponsored categories, usually called preferences, are capped at a total of 226,000 immigrants a year. Each of the preferences gets its own share of this total number. The first preference gets its share first; once all first preference applicants have been admitted, any admission slots left over from the first preference share are given to the second preference, and so on. Admissions are granted until all the applicants in all the preferences have been admitted, or until the cap of 226,000 admissions is reached.

The first preference includes the unmarried adult children of U.S. citizens. The first preference is allotted up to 23,400 admissions.

The second preference includes the spouses and unmarried adult children of lawful permanent residents. The second preference is allotted up to 114,200 admissions (plus any left over from above).

The third preference includes the married adult children of U.S. citizens. The third preference is allotted up to 23,400 admissions (plus any left over from above).

The fourth preference includes the siblings of U.S. citizens. The fourth preference is allotted up to 65,000 admissions (plus any left over from above).

Employment-Based Preferences

At present, the five employment-based preferences are capped at a total of 140,000 immigrants a year. Each of the preferences gets its own share of this total number. Any of the 140,000 admissions not used up by the employment-based preferences are given over to be used by the family-sponsored preferences.

The first preference is for priority workers. Priority workers include aliens with extraordinary ability in the sciences, arts, education, business, or athletics; outstanding professors and researchers; certain multinational executives and managers. The first preference is allotted up to 40,040 of the 140,000 admissions for the employment-based preferences.

The second preference is for the professionally advanced or exceptional. The second preference is allotted up to 40,040 of the 140,000 admissions for the employment-based preferences.

The third preference is for skilled workers, professionals, and needed unskilled workers.[79] The third preference is allotted up to 40,040 of the 140,000 admissions for the employment-based preferences.

The fourth preference is for certain special immigrants. Special immigrants include ministers of religion and other religious workers, and long-time alien employees of the U.S. government abroad. The fourth preference is allotted up to 9,940 of the 140,000 admissions for the employment-based preferences.

The fifth preference is for wealthy investors. The fifth preference is allotted up to 9,940 of the 140,000 admissions for the employment-based preferences.

It is important to realize that the dependent immediate relatives of those admitted to be employees are also counted as employment-based admissions.

The Visa Lottery

Lottery immigrants (also known as diversity program immigrants) are legal immigrants who are admitted because their countries are purported to be underrepresented in family-based and employment-based immigration.

Family-based immigration is based on the policy of giving preferential admission to applicants who have relatives already in the United States. Thus, the more immigrants there

---

[79] "Skilled workers" are defined as immigrants who are capable of performing skilled labor not of a temporary or seasonal nature, for which qualified workers are not available in the United States. "Professionals" are immigrants who hold baccalaureate degrees and who are members of the professions. "Unskilled workers" are immigrants capable of unskilled labo, for which qualified workers are not available in the United States.

are here from a country, the more people from that country are eligible to immigrate. As a result, the countries with large numbers of immigrants here squeeze out countries with fewer immigrants here. There are over two hundred countries in the world; yet six countries take 50% of the annual admissions to the U.S.

People not admitted through the family-based or employment-based programs may apply for the immigration "lottery." Nationals from all but a handful of countries are eligible. The lottery is a new program, established in 1990. Instead of lowering the number of other admissions to make room for the lottery, the lottery admissions were simply tacked on to the existing immigration levels. So the lottery adds 55,000 people to our annual immigration influx.

There are several problems with the lottery: it adds to the annual immigration level; it is random; it gives admission to illegal aliens; it enlarges the applicant backlog; it creates unrealistic expectations. The lottery picks only a few of the millions of people who apply, and it picks them at random. Some have questioned the policy basis of the lottery. People who are already here illegally are still eligible for the lottery. Since people who are here can more easily complete the application process, they have some advantage over those who are still in their home countries. Consequently, many of the lottery winners are in fact illegal aliens, who are then allowed to become legal immigrants.

Lottery immigrants usually have relatives back home. Once here, they can petition for those relatives to join them. As a result, the number of people eligible to immigrate rises, along with the number of people who do get in and the number of people waiting in the backlog. Over six million people apply for the lottery a year; only 55,000 win.

Refugees and Asylees

Refugees and asylees are aliens allowed to remain in the United States because they claim to face individual persecution from their home government. The difference between refuge and asylum lies in the location of the applicant; someone outside of the United States applies for refuge, whereas someone inside applies for asylum. Under U.S. law, there is no difference between the legal standard for refuge and the basis for asylum. Both are based on a claim of political persecution.

In recent years, the basis for refuge and asylum has often been forgotten. Refuge and asylum are for people who are persecuted as individuals by their government. It is not intended for people from countries where politics has created a difficult economy; for people who simply do not like the government of their home country or its burdens; for people who are being persecuted by someone other than their home government; for people whose governments are not particularly good at maintaining order; for people from societies that are not as enlightened as ours; or for people who would just plain prefer to be here than at home. If these were sufficient reasons for giving someone refuge or asylum, the standard would be unmanageable and unenforceable.

The number of refugees a year is limited informally by administrative agreement. The annual consultations between the State Department and the Congress have resulted in repeated increases over the last ten years. The asylum system is separate from the regular immigration system, and is almost entirely the creation of administrative regulation. While the regular system has some built-in limits, there is no limit to the number of people who can apply for asylum. Asylum applicants are allowed to remain in the U.S. while waiting for their claims to be decided. As a result, the number of asylum applications has increased dramatically in the last twenty years. In 1973, there were 1,913 asylum applications; in 1983, there were 26,091 asylum applications; in 1993, there were 150,014 asylum applications.

This increase is largely due to illegal aliens' increasing abuse of the asylum system as a mechanism for avoiding deportation. Illegal aliens who would otherwise be deported can file asylum applications, which must be processed before they can be deported. Many times, since such applicants are seldom held in custody, they disappear once they are released. Even if they pursue the asylum claim, that process, with many appeals and delays, can take years; by then, the illegal alien can claim that he has been in the United States so long that it would be a hardship to deport him. Such claims often succeed.

ILLEGAL ALIENS

There are essentially two kinds of illegal aliens:

- illegal entrants (who came into the country without inspection or permission).
- status violators (who came into the country with permission but who violate the conditions of their entry, or who enter through fraud of false pretenses).

It is important to realize that illegal aliens who enter the country legally and overstay their visas are as guilty of breaking immigration and criminal law as those who sneak past a border crossing guard; they constitute about half of the illegal alien population.

Do not confuse the number of illegal entrants with the number of illegal entries. Each time an alien illegal enters the U.S. it counts as an illegal entry; one person could enter the country many times over the year, and each time would constitute an illegal entry. For example, it is estimated that there are somewhere around 3,000,000 illegal entries every year; but that does not mean that there are 3,000,000 illegal entrants every year.

When most people talk about illegal aliens, they are talking primarily about illegal settlers. The INS estimates that about 300,000 illegal settlers come to the United States every year. The addition of these illegal settlers each year increases the overall number of illegal aliens residing in the United States. The estimated number of illegal settlers in the United States is around 5.3 million. Many people think that there are more illegal aliens in the country than legal aliens. That is not true. The number of legal aliens entering the country is usually at least three times larger than the number of illegal aliens.

Recommended Reading

Availability Codes:

B   Retail bookstores

S   Social Contract Press
316½ E. Mitchell Street, Suite 4
Petoskey, Michigan, 49770
Phone: (616) 347–1171
Fax: (616) 347–1185

F   The Federation for American Immigration Reform
Publication Department
1666 Connecticut Avenue, Suite 400
Washington, DC, 20009
Phone: (202) 328–7004
Fax: (202) 387–3447

Re-Charting America's Future: Responses to Arguments Against Stabilizing U.S. Population and Limiting Immigration, by Roy Beck, 1994, ISBN 1-881780-06-6. **S**
Drawing on the work of dozens of scientists, academics and other experts, this book examines the arguments used to justify the federal immigration policies that force U.S. population growth.

The Case Against Immigration, Roy Beck, 1995 (from W.W. Norton), ISBN 0-393-03915-3. **S B**
A powerful but compassionate manifesto for immigration reform, which lays out the country's moral obligations to reduce immigration.
Immigration By the Numbers, Roy Beck, 1996, ISBN1-881780-10-4. **S**

136

A videotape version of immigration expert Roy Beck's celebrated demonstration of the population consequences of current U.S. immigration policies that has been shocking audiences across the country.

Alien Nation: Common Sense About America's Immigration Disaster, Peter Brimelow, 1995 (from Random House), ISBN 0-679-43058-X. **B**

Brimelow's *Alien Nation* is not only the nation's best known and popular book on the need for immigration reform, but has been credited with opening the eyes of conservative America to the failures of modern immigration policy.

A Tale of Ten Cities: Immigration's Effect on the Family Environment in American Cities, Leon Bouvier & Scipio Garling, 1995, ISBN 0-935776-20-6. **F**

A daring comparison of high and low immigration cities, this study is the benchmark for examining immigration's impact on the quality of life in the United States.

Immigration 2000: The Century of the New American Sweatshop, 1992. **F**

This anthology of essays by national experts on economic and labor details the harm done by immigration policy to the American workforce.

Ten Steps to Ending Illegal Immigration, Jim Dorcy & Scipio Garling, 1995, ISBN 0-935776-16-8. **F**

The definitive blueprint for tackling illegal immigration, Ten Steps has inspired many of the recent reform in enforcing immigration law.

137

*You Can Help Reform Immigration: A Guide to Grassroots
Immigration Reform*, Jon Eifert & Scipio Garling, 1996,
ISBN 0-935776-21-4. **F**

This must-have manual is a how-to book on
becoming an activist in the growing movement for
immigration reform.

Resources

The Immigration Legislative Network (The ILN)

c/o FAIR
1666 Connecticut Avenue NW, Suite 400
Washington, DC, 20009

The ILN is the umbrella group for a host of local immigration reform organizations across the United States.

The Center for Immigration Studies (CIS)

1522 K Street NW, Suite 820
Washington, DC, 20005

CIS is a research center that studies immigration and its effect on all aspects of American life.

Negative Population Growth (NPG)

1608 20th Street NW #200
Washington, DC, 20009

NPG is a national membership organization that advocates a smaller U.S. population through responsible family planning and limiting immigration.

WEBSITES

THE IMMIGRATION AND NATURALIZATION SERVICE (INS)
http://www.usdoj.gov/ins

The INS site offers statistical information on the most recent year's immigrants, press releases, and other background information.

THE U.S. CENSUS BUREAU
http://www.census.gov/population/www/socdemo/foreign96.html

The U.S. Census Bureau presents data from the 1990 Census on the foreign-born, the 1996 Current Population Survey on the foreign-born, and population projections based on different immigration scenarios.

THE U.S. COMMISSION ON IMMIGRATION REFORM
http://www.utexas.edu/lbj/uscir

This site provides information on the work of the national bipartisan commission, which was established under the 1990 Immigration Act to study its effects.

THE SOCIAL CONTRACT
http://www.tscpress.com

The Social Contract offers in-depth studies on immigration and a host of related issues, such as population, language, assimilation, environment, national unity, and the balance between individual rights and civic responsibilities.

NEGATIVE POPULATION GROWTH

http://www.npg.org

NPG maintains a website on immigration as a population issue.

NUMBERS USA

http://www.numbersusa.com

Numbers USA offers evidence that today's record high immigration fuels rapid population growth, and a link for sending messages to Congress.

FEDERATION FOR AMERICAN IMMIGRATION REFORM

http://www.fairus.org

FAIR has the most comprehensive immigration website, including state-by-state immigration profiles and a daily summary of immigration news..

Index

How to S~~urvive~~ *Win* the Immigration Debate